Japanese Slang

Japanese Slang

UNCENSORED

Peter Constantine

YENBOOKS

YENBOOKS
2-6 Suido 1-chome, Bunkyo-ku, Tokyo 112, Japan

© 1994 by YENBOOKS

ISBN 0-8048-1942-4
LCC Card No. 94-60020

First edition, 1994

Printed in Japan

Contents

Acknowledgments

I WOULD like to express my deepest gratitude to the many individuals who over the years have provided me with the candid cultural information and the plain-spoken language data that were necessary for this book. I am especially grateful for the frankness with which they faced my grueling interrogations and for their generosity in offering to discuss private, personal, and often sensitive aspects of their life and work. Because of the delicate nature of their trade, many of the individuals who have contributed most to this book, have wished to remain incognito.

Among my American friends, I owe the greatest thanks to Burton Pike for his encouragement and inspiration, and for his constant advice and help. I am also grateful to my literary agent, Raphael Pallais, whose interest in medieval Japan proved to be most valuable, and to my editor Sally Schwager, whose profound knowledge of Japanese language and culture has been of great help.

I am grateful to Mark Peterson for sharing his intimate knowledge of the ins and outs of the New York street scene and its language. His analytic discussions of American street life helped me put my Japanese data into a Western perspective.

Among my Japanese friends, I owe special thanks to K. Inoue for the hours of sifting, dissecting, and analyzing the stacks of information that came pouring in, and to W. Ishida for our many frank discussions and for the many investigations that she tackled on my behalf. I am also thankful to N. Ichizono for her generous help, and to T. Yoshioka for her enthusiasm, encouragement, and for the fact-finding expeditions that she undertook.

I am especially grateful to the individuals who helped me in my research into slang expressions of ethnic Korean and Chinese extraction: I would like to thank L. Kim, S. Yang, and J. Ma, and Mr. Park, whose intimate knowledge of both the Korean and the Japanese scene helped me track the etymology of some of the more sinuous Japanese-Korean expressions.

Finally, a very special word of thanks to Dr. Lundquist, Chief Librarian of the Oriental Division of the New York Public Library, and to Ms. Kim, Section Head of the East Asian Division, whose scholarly council and advice on Japanese and Korean publications were of great help.

Introduction

CURIOUS FOREIGNERS who prowl the darkest alleys of Tokyo, who dart into secret red-light bars in Osaka, or bolt up the stairs of the corrugated slum brothels near the port of Yokohama, quickly realize that there is much more to the Japanese language than meets the ear. What they have stumbled on are Japan's fascinating secret languages: the *ingo* (hidden words) or *ago* (jaw) used by looters, car heisters, prostitutes, pimps, bag snatchers, muggers, and wallet swipers. As one descends deeper and deeper into the Japanese underworld, the language becomes more potent and rich in clandestine trade words and covert metaphors.

At the street level, everyone uses the same rough and unbridled slang. But by the time the sub rosa crowd secretly congregates in its back-alley clubs and bars, each group slips into its own exclusive, razor-fine argot. Secrecy is of paramount importance: delicate heists need to be mapped out, strategies analyzed, financial matters discussed, illegitimate meetings set up, and bands of looters returning from a successful stint might want to recap their triumph over a few loud and festive drinks. What, however, if the person who is quietly nursing a drink at the end of the bar is *aori*—an undercover cop?

One wrong word can unleash a shower of hand-cuffs.

It has been this professional need for utter discretion that has played the most important role in the fast-paced development of Japan's "hidden" languages. A careful criminal will linguistically only trust his or her closest peers, which is why bagsnatcherese is so different from pickpocketese, and why brothel, sex-bathhouse, and massage-parlor talk, although closely related, will veer off and become unintelligible when hot technicalities are broached.

Another important reason for the heated development of underworld slang has been the day-to-day need for special criminal trade expressions. Japanese looter slang, for instance, stocks its lexicon with long lists of labyrinthine terms, ranging from hundreds of nouns for house doors and alarm systems to verbs covering every conceivable method of breaking and entering. The lock specialists, on the other hand, have a name for every segment of a lock or a bolt, and strings of exotic words for lock-picking needles, master keys, and the top, bottom, or side sections of tumbler pins. Pickpocketing verbs can name every larcenous flick of the wrist, and special nouns specify wallets by their position in a pocket, their size, the visibility of their outline through the trouser material, the degree of their emptiness or fullness, and whether they are brimming over with bills, or merely heavy with small change.

The other important initiative behind the growth of Japan's secret slang has been the herd instinct, defined in trendy Japanese as *uii-izumu* (we-ism). Japanese criminals prefer to operate out of an association or gang, in which private language or jargon becomes the invisible club badge. To be one of the boys you first of all have to speak like one of the boys. When teenage roughnecks are initiated into the bottom ranks of a gang they frantically imitate the dashing language of their power-wielding elders, who themselves had imitated the locution of their elders. When youngsters join a criminal association they immediately cleanse their vocabulary of all trendy English words and jingly adolescent expressions, and adopt the gang's tough and mature vernacular. It is this orthodox traditionalism in the Japanese underworld that has led it to conserve long-forgotten medieval and even pre-medieval expressions. A *shin-tabukuro* (money sack) is still a wallet on Tokyo's streets, just as it used to be in the good old samurai days, and a *shintagamari* (from *shinta kamari*, "the money lunges in") is still a wallet that is brimming over with cash. Some groups call a snooping policeman Sakubei, the name of some medieval lawman, while a long-forgotten idiot, Kinjūrō, is still invoked in criminal circles as an unpleasant insult.

When gangs bring up sexual organs, elegant and elaborate ancient words abound. *Kintare* (golden dangle) and *suzuko* (bell child) are general synonyms for testicles, while *katakin* (side gold) is the one testicle that dangles visibly lower than the other. *Kenke* (pickles) refers to scrota that pull themselves up into stiff small balls during arousal.

In the West, we expect slang to change with every high school graduation class. What is new is decided in teenage circles, and we turn to the MTV channel to keep up with the seasonal changes. We find out that "Whoops, there it is!" was the summer-of-1993 term for "Nice ass!" or "Gosh, her shorts are short!" For an introduction to American street speech, we tune our sets to the post-L.A.-riot tirades of youthful West Coast gang members. As round after round of unintelligible phrases pour out, we are increasingly convinced that slang is an impenetrable, if transient, mechanism of the young.

On Japan's streets, however, it is the older criminal generation, the men in power, who decide what words are in and what words are out. New slang must be constantly conjured up, as the streetwise Japanese police eagerly snatch up all the clandestine expressions they can find. The captured words then make their way into the police's own private jargon, with the result that what is fashionable in the underworld one season is bandied about in police boxes the next.

But where do illegal brothel associations, pickpocketing leagues, bands of looters, drug pushers, and pink-salon masseuses turn to for new words?

One favorite method is to take existing slang words and revamp them with new associations. *Teka* (bright), for instance, has been used for generations on Tokyo's streets to mean "fire," and soon arson came to be known as *teka o tsukeru* (adding the bright), which then changed into a dialectized *deka o tsukeru*. The next playful step was *tekkari* (twinkle): robbing and then torching the building to cover one's tracks. Then *tekkari* took on the meaning "summer," then "unseasonably hot," then just plain "it's hot today, isn't it?" The most irreverent use of *tekkari* has been for matches:

- *Oi, tekkari motteru ka?*
  Yo, you got matches?

An even quicker method of creating a neologism is to invert existing words, rendering them incomprehensible in quick speech. This characteristic is also prevalent in French, Argentinian Spanish, Korean, Hindi, Indonesian, and Javanese street slangs. *Kōhii* (coffee), and *baibai* (bye bye), are playfully flipped over into *hikkō* and *ibaiba*. On a grittier level, *chinpo* (penis) becomes *pochin*, *shiroi* ("white," i.e. cocaine) becomes *roishi*, *hero* (heroin) becomes *roha*, and *keibu* (police) becomes *bukei*. This trend, known as *gyakugo* (topsy-turvy words) is often taken further than just simple syllabic reversal. *Yato*, for instance, a malignant street word for razor, sprung from *yatoko*, which is the inversion of *tokoya* (barber shop). The case of how the southern Japanese town of Shimonoseki became a popular train station-thief word for luggage involves an even knottier web of word changes. The standard *kaban* (bag) was first reversed into *banka*, which then developed into *bakan*. The station crowd looked at the new word and realized that it could be written with the characters *ba* (horse) and *kan* (barrier), the same character used for the *noseki* portion of the town of Shimonoseki.

This art of capsizing words, however, had been quickly mastered by the police, and the street crowd set out to marshal new expressions of a more covert nature. The handiest source of impenetrable words turned out to be the ethnic Korean and Chinese gangsters who had poured into the Japanese underworld in the post-World War II years. The abrupt

Korean word for dog *(kē)* came to mean "police," while *kujuri* was used as a secret Korean word for "money," *hōza* for "wallet," and *higehachiya* for "murder." No Japanese policeman, the gangsters argued, could possibly guess that *tējitari*, Korean for "pig's leg," means gun. The Chinese words, the Japanese gangsters felt, were even more exotic: *tsuō maimai*, Chinese for "going into business," came to mean "looting," and *ryahiyatan*, Chinese for "swatting insects," was redirected to mean "blasting down walls."

Another swift way of replenishing a criminal lingo's lexicon was to bring in provincial dialect words. In Japan, vocabulary, speech patterns, and accents are liable to change from one village to the next, which guarantees that any novel words brought in from distant provinces will nonplus even the most cunning eavesdropper. *Eri o tsukeru*, for instance, to the untrained Japanese ear means "to wear a collar." But in Tokyo's breaking-and-entering circles, it came to mean "picking locks," an expression that trickled down to the big city from northeastern Japan. *Sanpira* (lock) and *geri* (widget) are reputed to have been borrowed from Wakayama dialects, while *pika* (to flick open a switchblade) came from the Yamaguchi dialect.

The dialect words have made their strongest impact on red-light speech. Sexual organs from every corner of Japan have managed to make their way down into metropolitan sex bars, brothels, bathhouses, and massage parlors. An interesting twist of Japanese semantics which has brought many a brothel conversation to a screeching halt, is that what is the word for a female organ in one part of a province might turn into a testicle a few miles down the road, and then a few miles further down become a penis.

I had originally planned *Japanese Slang Uncensored* as a tough, reveal-it-all sequel to my first language book, *Japanese Street Slang*. My intention had been to reveal more of these tough forbidden street words that could never slither under the blocks of a self-respecting printing press. But as I continued moving down in Japanese society from interview to interview, I became fascinated with what my word suppliers did for a living. The deeper I slipped, the stronger the speakers' personality and modus vivendi shone through the words. Making a dazzling list of alphabetized taboo terms might be fun and linguistically rewarding, but I realized that in order to really get to the roots of the slang I would also have to dig down to the social foundation of the group I was listening to.

As I began writing *Japanese Slang Uncensored* I became increasingly convinced that the strongest slang would pale if it were not presented along with its speakers. I decided to use these secret, "hidden words" to reveal the shadowy sections of Japanese society that few upstanding Japanese and even fewer Westerners ever have the opportunity to explore.

1 ▪ Japanese Thieves

IN THE darker corners of Japan's street scene, till tappers, pickpockets, heistmen, and bank crackers are tightly knit, along with thieves of every description, into a web of underworld associations and networks. Age-old street hierarchies still prevail, and modern Japanese thieves, much like modern Japanese businessmen, are classed according to their experience, track record, age—and whom they know. Some criminal corporations are rich; their *eriito* (elite) or top executives govern ten, twenty, and even thirty city blocks with an iron fist. Other groups are shoddy and small and work out of a street or alley, snatching handbags, lifting wallets, and stripping cars. But whatever their rank or affiliation, professional purloiners would be outraged should they be referred to as *dorobō* (thieves), *settō* (larcenists), *gōtō* (burglars), or *oihagi* (robbers).

- *Agari da'tte, tondemo nē! Ore wa akainu da ze!*
  Me, a riser? No way! I'm a red dog!
  (Me, climb into houses? No way! I'm an arsonist!)

Newcomers to the Japanese street soon realize that

thieves come in two sizes: the *shinobikomi*, "those who enter crawling" (smooth criminals who work with circumspection), and the *odorikomi*, "those who enter dancing" (brash criminals with guns). While successful dancers are applauded for their devil-may-care recklessness, the experienced crawler is admired for the light-fingered strategy with which he or she will calculate a heist. A house is chosen, inhabitants watched, police movements in the neighborhood monitored, and locks and alarm systems studied. When a crawler finally moves in on his target he carefully accounts for the weather, the time, and the presence or absence of a victim.

Crawling

In classical criminal slang an unattended house full of choice loot was referred to as *akisu* (empty nest), and "crawling" thieves who specialized in these houses were secretly known as *akisunerai* (empty-nest targeters). But the police uncovered the word, adopted it, and soon began using it in official reports. *Akisunerai* spread like wild fire. It was snatched up by newspapers, detective novels, gangster movies, cartoons, and finally even dictionaries.

With *akisunerai* flushed out of hiding, new code words appeared on the streets. Empty houses were rebaptized *nukesu* (void nests), *nuke* for short, and *ai* (chance). Tokyo's Korean gangsters introduced their own exotic word, *hotsuraiki*. The more theatrical thieves took to calling their empty houses *butai* (stage). A sneak thief, they argued, could always guarantee a spectacular entry, a breathtaking performance, and a dashing exit. Some gangs took the thespian idea even further and began referring to breaking and entering as *butai o fumu* (stepping onto the stage) and even *butai e kamaru* (barging onto the stage).

- *Yappa shū ni sankai ijō butai o fumu mon ja nai yo— tama n'ya rerakkusu shinē to.*
  You know I really wouldn't step on stage more than three times a week—one has to relax too, you know.
- *Aitsu ga butai o funda no wa, are ga saigo datta no sa.*
  That was the last time he stepped onto the stage.
- *Aitsu ja butai e kamaru'tte koto ga dō yū koto nan no ka chitto mo wakatcha inē!*
  He really has no idea what barging onto the stage is all about!
- *Asu ore ga butai e kamaru no o matte miro yo!*
  Just you wait till I barge onto that stage tomorrow!

The crawlers and sneak thieves who barged into these houses were also given new names. They reappeared as *nukeshi* (void specialists), *nuke-chan* (little Mr. Void), *akishi* (empty specialists), *kisukai* (from *akisukai*, "empty-nest buyer"), *sukai* (nest buyers), and, more elegantly, *gaikōin* (commercial travelers). *Shinobi* (creeping into) was molded into a whole line of new words. *Shinobishi* (creep specialist) became the rage and after the police adopted it, it was pruned down to *nobi* and *nobishi* (*nobi*-master), and then, for optimum security, was further disguised as *nobe* and *nobeshi*.

The law, however, was quick to pick up on these words too, and feverish bands of burglars churned out ever more outlandish expressions. Sneak thieves became *yaya* (house-ters), *yashiya* (mansion-ers), *tobi* (kites), *konchū* (bugs), and *sagashi* (seekers). Some clans even resorted to effervescent nonsensical names like *zabu* (bubbles), *nagajirashi* (long teasers), and *nagashari* ("noodles," a word of dubious Buddhist priestly origin, literally "long Buddha's bones"). The idea that many of the older diehard professionals had the habit of carefully tiptoeing from room to room in their socks gave rise to the jejune quip *shirotabi* (white tabi-socks—traditional socks that younger and more fashion-conscious criminals would not be caught dead stealing in). In naughtier cliques, the now standard expression for sneak thief, *akisunerai* (empty-nest targeter), has been flipped into a rebarbative *ketsunerai* (ass targeter) and *ketsusagashi* (ass searcher). The logic behind this witty switch is that *ketsu* (ass) and *ana* (hole) are written with the same character. A sneak thief, the gangsters argue, prods about in the dark searching for a hole to enter.

The even earthier criminals go all out and refer to breaking and entering as *kamahoru* (ass fucking) and burglars as *kamahori* (ass fuckers).

- *Aitsu mo karekore ketsunerai yatte yonjū nen kā!*
  Well, he's been an ass targeter for forty years now!
- *Ketsusagashi'tte no wa mattaku hone no oreru shigoto da ze!*
  Being an ass searcher is real stressful, you know!
- *Kamahoru nante ore mo iya da yo! Shikashi uchi nya kakā to gaki ga matte yagaru kara na!*
  I've had it with ass fucking! But what can I do, I have a wife and kids at home!
- *Ano Kōbe kara kita kamahori nakanaka yaru na.*
  That ass fucker from Kobe's real good.

Chaster bands have given their boys the swash-buckling names of the legendary neighborhood criminals of yesteryear. Tayū, Tōbe, Kanpei, or Sansho serve as practical synonyms in everyday gang jargon. The names of shoddier ancestors have also survived on the streets. These are doled out to sneak thieves who are less successful, such as Gonkichi, for individuals who never manage to pull off a hefty job, Gonsuke, for maladroit and bedraggled criminals who live from hand to mouth, and Heikurō, for sneak thieves who, barely escaping from a botched-up job, are in hiding.

Gangs with a high ethnic Korean membership went in for a simpler linguistic solution. While their all-Japanese counterparts scraped for clever new secret terms, these gangs simply peppered their clandestine speech with exotic Korean expressions. Sneak thieves were given long and impenetrable names that were sure to baffle even the most streetwise police unit: *chimūruhetsuta*, *banchiorutokii*, *kutsuharakachiya*, and *konkurusarubisa*. Some of the more pronounceable Korean gang-words for stealers, such as *sangui* (mouse), the hybrid *chiuya* (*chiu*, Korean for "rat," and *ya*, Japanese for "guy"), and *kē* (hound) made the broader national scene.

- *Isoge yo! Shita de Kawasaki no kutsuharakachiya omē no koto matteru ze!*
  Hurry up! That heister from Kawasaki is waiting downstairs for you!
- *Goji ni rei no konkurusarubisa to au tehazu da.*
  We're supposed to meet that heister guy at five.

After World War II, downtown Tokyo gangs had

become ethnically even more diverse as hordes of eager Chinese youths spilled out of the tightly knit Chinatowns of Yokohama and Osaka. Both Japanese and Korean gangsters were charmed by the exotic vocabularies these new conscripts brought with them. Breaking into a house was given the pounding name *hākoyau* (banging at the furnace), which was inspired by the Japanese burglary words *tonton* (bang bang) and *kanamono* (ironmongery). The new secret words for burglar were *honpa* (from *heng pa*, "unconscionable snatcher"), *chiin-chende* (hard-cash-taker) and *yauchienu* (from *yao qien*, "wanting money"). *Chiipaishu'ende* became the alternative word for sneak thief, and *ninkātā* (he who leaves no traces) was reserved for cream-of-the-crop master thieves.

- *Shinmai no hākoyau umaku yatteru kai?*
  How's your new ironmonger working out?
- *Ano honpa itsumo hitori de shigoto o yaru no sa.*
  You know, that unconscionable snatcher always works alone.
- *Ore wa tekkiri ano chiin-chende wa kono hen no koto shitteru to omottan da ga nā!*
  Man, I thought that hard-cash-taker knew the neighborhood!
- *Oi, chotto kore mite miro yo! Kono ate wa Ōsaka no ninkātā kara te ni ireta mono da ze!*
  Yo, take a look at this one! I got this door jagger from an Osaka pro!

Along with ethnic diversity came the initial wave of lock-picking and safe-cracking burglaresses. The first female mob bosses had begun ruling their streets with an iron fist, buying, selling, and even marrying their way up the violently masculine hierarchy of the Japanese underworld. In 1982 the struggle for criminal gender empowerment reached new heights when the gentle and soft-spoken Taoka Fumiko maneuvered herself onto the throne of Japan's largest and most powerful mob-syndicate, the Yamaguchi gang. With the first signs of equal employment opportunity, the toughest and most belligerent women mingled with their local sneak thief crowd and soon began acquiring their own *sanyabukuro* (widget bags), in which they could neatly arrange their own tools of the sneak-thieving trade: *koburi* (master keys), *harigane* (wire-jiggers), *neji* (crowbars), *hōchō* ("kitchen cleavers," or lock-breaking wrenches), and *aka* ("red," or blow torch). This first generation of female professional burglars has been given a jargon name of Chinese gang extraction, *būē* (the maternal ones).

Lootable homes were also ordered into strict categories. For instance, a house that is always left unattended in the morning is *asa aki* (morning empty), while *hinaka* (broad daylight), and *hiru'kisu* (noontime empty-nest) are good midday targets.

- *Asa aki bakkari to omotetan da nā! Chhe! Poka shichimatta!*
  I thought that house was always empty in the mornings! Man was I wrong!
- *Nagahama-dōri wa hinaka darake datta no shitteta ka?*
  Did you know that Nagahama Street is full of empty houses at lunch time?

A quick noon job is known as *hirumai* (noontime dance), *tentō* (heavenly road), or *nitchū o fumu* (stepping on broad daylight). Thieves who work exclusively during lunch hours call themselves *hishi* (day masters), *nitchūshi* (broad-daylight specialists), *hiruwashi* (noontime eagles) or, in downtown Tokyo, *shirotobi*. The origin of the word *shirotobi* has sparked great controversy among the gangs. Some maintain that it means "white kite," others "white cape," others still "white pilferer." In his book *Ingo Kotoba no Kuruizaki*, the renowned linguist Umegaki Minoru argues that the *shiro* of *shirotobi* is really just a bastardization of *shiru*, the Tokyo-dialect word for lunchtime (*hiru*). The elegant *shirotobi*, he decrees, is none other than the modest *hirutombi* (lunchtime pilferer).

Homes that are regularly left defenseless in the evening are ranked as *yoiaki* (nightfall empty), and more poetically as *bankei* (evening scenery), and evening thieves call their sprees *yoimatsuri* (nightfall festivals), *koigamari* (dark crawls), *yoigamari* (evening crawls), and *yoarashi* (night intrusion).

- *Yoiaki da to omotte shinobikonda no ni, babā ga neteru no mitsukete tamagechimatta ze!*
  I broke in thinking it was a nightfall empty, but this old bitch was asleep inside. Man, you should have seen me freak!
- *Koko futaban no yoimatsuri wa mattaku hisan datta ze!*
  The last two nighttime festivals were a total flop!
- *Kinō no ban wa koigamari ni wa chotto samusugi da ze.*
  Last night was a bit too cold for a dark crawl.

Professionals who specialize in late-night thievery are known on street corners as *kōmori* (bats), *taka* (hawks), *yonaki* (night cries), *yashō* (night businessmen), *yonashi* (night specialists), and *anma* (traditional blind masseurs—they work in the dark, feeling their way around). *Fuke* (staying up late) is also used, along with nimble variations such as *fukenin* (stay-up-late person), and *fukeshi* (stay-up-late specialist). But heavy criminal jargon, in constant fear of police discovery, calls its nocturnal thieves *tatonuhowa* (blowing out the candle), *pūtairen* (uninvolved guy), *honteinu* (confused in the dark), *yauren* (servant gang), and *teinshin* (by starlight), words of ethnic Chinese extraction, and *kipuntoi*, *chinsa*, and *sūsūyotsu*, of ethnic Korean background.

- *Aitsu wa anma ni wa chotto toshi ga ikisugiteru ze.*
  He's getting to be a bit old to be a blind masseur.
- *Oi, hora, are o mite miro yo! Kōmori ga yojinobotteru ze!*
  Yo, man, take a look at that! Look at that bat scamper up!
- *Oi, miro yo! Ano futari no chinsa wa Kawasaki ni sunderun da ze!*
  Yo, look there! Those two night thieves live in Kawasaki!
- *Ano onna ga kono atari dewa ichiban no sūsūyotsu da'tte koto omae shitteta kai?*
  That woman there, did you know she's the best night thief around here?

Thieves who go on walks looking for eligible houses are said to be flowing (*nagasu*). During these flows, buildings are carefully appraised and classed according to potential loot, lighting, street exposure, and the accessibility of front and back entrances and windows. Likely looking houses are earmarked as *anzan* ("easy deliveries," as in birth) or *andon* (flimsy lanterns), while buildings that offer easy entry but are dangerously close to busy roads or police stations are rated as *gan kitsui* (the eyes are tough), and more lyrically *oki ga kurai* (the seascape is dark).

- *Nante kot'a! Koko wa anzen no hazu datta no ni, aitsu tsukamachimatta ze!*
  What the fuck! This was meant to be an easy job and he got busted!
- *Iyāā! Nanda kono hen, zenbu andon ja nē ka? Kor'a boro mōke da ze!*
  Man! Fuckin'-A! This area is full of easy houses! We're really gonna cash in!
- *Kono hen wa gan kitsui kara, saketa hō ga ii ze.*
  Avoid this neighborhood. The eyes are tough.
- *Hā! Kono yakata wa meppō ii ga, oki ga kurai ze.*
  What a beautiful, stately mansion. Pity the seascape's so dark.

After flowing past house after house, the thieves close in on the most suitable target in three phases. *Toba o kimeru* (choosing the den) is the preliminary audition, in which whole rows of homes are given a general glance-over. *Toba o tsunagu* (tethering the den) is the second, closer look in which alarm systems and entry and exit points are examined. The final stage is *toba o fumu* (stepping on the den): out of all the possible targets, one home is chosen, and the thief approaches it, tool bag in hand. Once a house has been picked, the thieves proclaim *ate ga tsuku* (the aim will be fulfilled), and it graduates from being a *toba* (den) to a *taisaki*, pronounced by some groups *daisaki* (the table ahead).

Many of the better burglar gangs employ individuals who make a career of spotting vulnerable houses.

In the post-war years in Tokyo these men and women came to be known as *doroya* (streetsters) and *hiki* (pullers), while in Osaka and Kyoto they were given the pastoral title of *hitsujimawashi* (meandering sheep). The gang would pay them *tsukesage* (touchdown), the cab- and bus-fare from one location to the next, and if they spotted a good house would guarantee them *kabu* (stocks), a share in the loot. As criminals became more and more affluent during the sixties, seventies, and eighties, the *kurumaebi*, or prawns (literally "car shrimps"), moved in on the scene. These were the modern "streetsters" and "pullers," who combed their areas by car. Spotting a prime target, they would whip out their car phone, and crouching secretively (hence the "shrimp"), would quickly beep a burglar.

Thieves who work alone are known as *ichimaimono* (one sheet of individual). Some are completely independent of larcenous attendants; others have sturdy gang affiliations but do breaking and entering on their own. Thieves who work in pairs are classed as *nimaimono* (two sheets of individual), in threes, *sanmaimono* (three sheets of individual), and in foursomes, *yonmaimono* (four sheets of individual).

- *Aitsu wa shōgai ichimaimono de tōsō'tten dakara, mattaku hen na yatsu da ze!*
  He's real weird; he's been a loner all along.
- *Shigoto wa nimaimono de yaru ni koshita kot'ā nē yo!*
  You've gotta be at least a twosome to carry off a job well! (*kot'ā* is Tokyo slang for *koto wa*)
- *Ore-tachi mo sanmaimono de hajimete nagai koto naru nā.*
  It's been ages since we started working as a threesome.

- *Ore-tachi no nawabari ni ano yonmaimono ga shima tsukurō to shiteru rashii ze!*
  It looks like those four guys are trying to move in on our territory.

Groups that work under the umbrella of a gang report directly to the *kaoyaku* (face function), who is also lovingly referred to as the *kataoya* ("one parent," as in one-parent family). This parent is like a department manager in a bona fide firm: he hires and fires executives and maneuvers them profitably from one job to the next. When the ringleader happens to be a younger man, mischievous executives might refer to him behind his back as *anigao* (brother face). In his presence, however, heads are brusquely bowed and he is meekly addressed as *aniki* (older brother). When sneak thieves work in packs, social and professional hierarchy plays a star role. The man in charge is *dotama*, a name the street crowd claims developed from *atama* (head). The *dotama* is the brain of the pack. He might not personally break the lock, smash the window, or climb the drainpipe, but he makes the on-location decisions, orchestrating each movement of the burglary. In rougher packs the leader is the *konatruki*, a Korean gang word for "ruffian" which has acquired on Tokyo's modern streets a whiff of bravura and daredevilry. Important jobs that promise a high yield in loot are handled by larger sneak-thieving groups that come equipped with specialized watchmen, lockbreakers, computerized-alarm dismantlers, and a vault cracker or two.

Partners in crime refer to each other as *hikiai* (those who pull against each other), *tsute* (connections), *dōshi* (kindred spirits), *gui* and *guhi* (lopped-off versions of

tagui, "peer"), *hōbai* (comrade), and more affection-
ately as *kyōdai* (brothers) which, for security, is often
inverted to the less comprehensible *daikyō*. Cruder
bands of thieves, however, opt for heftier appella-
tions. A favorite is the Korean expression *chie*, which
is often distorted to a more feral *chiyē* or *chiyā*. The
general rule with this set of words is: the harsher the
expression, the warmer the criminal bond. *Busuke*
(plug ugly), *fushiyaburi* (joint breaker), *hiru* (leech),
and *hine* (stale) are often used with great cordiality by
one leathery tough to another.

- *Nan da yo? Orera no hikiai wa anna chatchii doa mo
  akerarenē'n da ze?*
  What the fuck? Our buddy can't even open a simple
  door like this?
- *Orera wa dōshi kamo shirenē ga, aitsu wa dōmo mushi
  ga sukanē.*
  We might be partners, but somehow I just don't
  like the guy.
- *Oi! Oi kā-chan! Chotto soko de chiyā to hikkakete kuru
  wa!*
  Yo! Hey old woman! I'm just going out for a bit
  with the gang!
- *Oi, busuke yo! Katai koto iwazu ni—mō ippai tsukiae
  yo!*
  C'mon butt-face, cut the crap and let's have an-
  other drink!
- *Oi tanomu ze! Omae ore no fushiyaburi ja nē ka? Kane
  kashite kure yo!*
  C'mon man, you're my partner, man! Lend me the
  money!
- *Ōsaka no hine ichiban tayori ni naru ze.*
  Our most reliable men are the guys from Osaka.

Another important part of respectable sneak-thieving gangs are the assistants, usually younger men who do dirty work like *terikiri* ("burning and cutting," or blowtorching locks) and *kaminari* ("thunderbolt," or making entry holes in roofs). These assistants are called *tobakiri* (den cutters) and *ashi* (legs), and are usually studying hard to become full-fledged professionals themselves. The youngest in the group, who is kept busy carrying tool bags and loot, is the *hidarisode* (left sleeve). He keeps out of the way, trotting behind the experienced elder of the group, the *migisode* (right sleeve), and drinks in as much technique as circumstances allow.

In a class of his own, the gang's lookout stands inconspicuously at gates, ducking into apartment house entrances or waiting in the getaway car, his hand on the ignition key. The lookouts of old whistled at the first sign of danger and were often masters at imitating tremulous bird calls; today's professionals, however, beep, page, and even ring up the gang on cellular phones. Over the years thousands of thief clans, large and small, have invented throngs of inspired cognomens for their watchmen. The lookouts' job was to keep their eyes peeled, what the Japanese call "stretched." *Gan o haru* (he is stretching his eyes) came to mean "he's keeping lookout for us," as did *toibaru* (he is stretching far). The men themselves became *ganhari* (eye stretchers), *toibari* (far stretchers), and then *kenshi* (see masters), *tōmi* (far lookers), *banmen* (watching faces), and *higemi* ("mustache watchers," or cop watchers). Some gangs even billed them with the dashing title *yariban* (spear guard). As the lookout men made it their job to peek over walls, peer through partitions, and spy over fences and railings, they came to be known as *takanyūdō* (tall giants). Another favorite has been *otenkinagashi* (the weather flows). Like a weatherman, the lookout watches for the slightest change in the atmosphere.

The most popular criminal word for watchmen of the sixties and seventies was *tachiko* (standing child), an expression which, to the plunderers' chagrin, was then swiped by the red-light crowd, to be used as a jocular word for prostitute. The thieves quickly flushed *tachiko* from their vocabularies.

Breaking into a Tokyo Mansion

A mansion has been chosen, the neighborhood inspected, and the date and time of the break-in set. The final word from the boss is: *Yoshi! Mimai ni iku to shiyō!* "That's it! We'll definitely pay that respectful visit." Those who will go on this visit gather in a process dubbed by gang jargon as *wa ni naru* (becoming a ring). A sophisticated group will hold a board meeting to discuss the delicate technicalities of the project. Here each crook has the opportunity to bring his or her expertise to the table in what is defined as *ueshita o tsukeru* (up and down together). Sipping tea, the group will verbally climb up the mansion's walls, down its drainpipes, across railings, and over roofs. In some clans this is called *tanka o tsukusu* (trying all the doors).

Then the looters leave the discussion table and begin arranging their tool bags, polishing their jiggers and oiling their widgets. The solemn act of dropping the tools one by one into the bag is called *netabai* (from *neta hai*, "the seeds enter"). The careful thief will chose staple instruments like *yōji* (lock picks), *rokkupari* (lock jiggers), *dosu* (wrench knives), *geri* (jaggers), *sori* (blades, from *kamisori*, "razor"), and a set of *nezumi* ("mice," or master keys). When the bags are ready, the time for *fumitsukeru* (attaching the steps) has come. Last minute phone calls are made, precautionary guns might be loaded, and, should they run into a domestic animal on the job, pork cutlets laced with cyanide are wrapped up in aluminium foil. These meat packages are wittily known as either *shisankin* (monetary contributions) or *tsukaimono* (wrapped gifts).

Arriving on the scene, the thieves hastily do *suzume* (sparrow), a quick check of surrounding streets and alleys for police patrols. If the coast is clear, the house is approached and the clan does *atekomi* (aim fulfillment), in which it might peek into the garage to see if the inhabitants' cars are there, or look to see which windows are lit.

A gate that has been carelessly left unlocked is baptized *chūyā*, a word of Korean pedigree. If the gate is locked, but so flimsily that a swift prod will unhinge it, the looters will murmur *marumage* (the traditional knotted hairstyle of a married woman—pull one pin out and ornaments and tresses come tumbling down). A gate that is securely locked is called by all-male gangs *maekake onna* (aproned woman): a man wishing to enter must first rip her apron off. In this case, the lock will either be picked (*koburu*), wrenched open (*shiburu*), or blowtorched in a process known as *kamaboko* (fish paste) and *yakikiri* (burn cut). If the lock proves too formidable, then the gang will go for *monbarai* (gate disposal) or *monbarashi* (gate dispelling). Gate butts, metal straps, pins, springs, and hinge shutters are snipped and wrenched, and the gate is lifted off its hinges.

Agile clans, however, might simply go for a quick *kaburu* (scampering over the wall), also known in more theatrical cliques as *maku o koeru* (getting beyond the stage curtains). While the group's agile youngsters nimbly hoist themselves over barriers of brick or wire, the more weatherworn professionals rely on either their octopus (*tako*), a rope ladder with iron hooks on top, or the more portable *minjaku* (knotted rope). These men and women call wall climbing *yama ni noboru* (climbing the mountain) or *yamagoshi* (going over the mountain), a term that is frowned upon by criminal women, as it also means violent rape.

When the robbers are on the premises the macho sexual imagery continues. They have had to fiddle with the locks, tinker with the hinges, twiddle the screws, and putter the latches. The gate and wall, they argue, are as difficult to handle as an unyielding woman. Even the most manful of men has to struggle to perform the crucial *maemakuri* ("lifting the skirt from the front," meaning the thieves enter through the front gates), or the even more crucial *shirimakuri* ("lifting the skirt from behind," as in the gate or fence is at the rear of the house).

- *Maemakuri hotondo ichijikan mo kakechimatta ze!*
  It took almost an hour to get those skirts hitched up (to break through those front gates)!
- *Anna inakamon' ga shirimakuri dekiru wake nē darō!*
  You expect that village yokel to know how to hitch up a skirt from behind (to break through a back gate)?

- *Omae yamagoshi no mae ni wa, maemakuri shina yo nā!*
  Man! You don't just rape her straight out—you
  have to hitch up those skirts first!
  (Don't just climb the wall—try the gates first!)

When visiting one of the better mansions, a looter
has to be prepared for what is known in back alleys as
a *muzukashii* (a difficult), the pedigreed guard dog. A
beast that starts barking and snarling ferociously is
gabinta, a word of Korean descent, meaning "it has no
respect for its superiors." If a "here doggy doggy!"
followed by an attempt to pat the animal does not
calm it, most thieves will bring out the deadly pork
chop. This is known as *inukoro o abuseru* (injuring the
mutt), or more sardonically *shūtome o kudoku* (silenc-
ing one's mother-in-law).

A careful rabble of thieves will now take a final
outside look at the house. Are there any hidden com-
puterized alarm systems, cameras, or infra-red contraptions (*sekigaisen*)? Professionals stress the
importance of following strict looting procedures with
an eye to Japan's brisk technological advances.

The cautioning proverb often quoted outside the
targeted homes is:

- *Ushi no kuso demo dandan.*
  Even a cow shits plop by plop.

Younger bandits who storm their mansions without the perpetual checking and rechecking of the
premises are branded by their elders as *parrari* (fool-
ish ones). The youngsters throw back at the streetwise
cow proverb the classical rejoinder:

- *Yōjin ni shiro horobizu.*
  A fortress can not be stormed cautiously.

A looter of substance skulks around the house one last time. This final precaution is called "swimming" (*oyogu*), "sidling" (*oyoru*), or "flower listening" (*kiku no hana*). If there is the slightest sign of danger, there is still time to safely abort the mission.

The burglars will have chosen a house amenable to the method of breaking and entering that they prefer. On the streets all these professionals are *akisunerai* (empty-nest targeters), but when they finally crawl into a yard with widgets, tweezers, and window jiggers in hand, they acquire more specific names.

Some of the more athletic individuals, for instance, are known as *agari* (ascenders), *nobi* (climbers), *ete* (monkeys), and *kumo* (spiders). They scamper over hedges and walls and onto balconies, usually entering the house from the top floor and working their way down. The thieves' jargon secretly calls its roofs *neya* (a simple inversion of the standard word for roof, *yane*), or *ten* (heaven) and roof windows are called *nekoiri* (cat entrances). A wall is *beka* (an inversion of the regular word for wall, *kabe*), and the thief's standard word for door is *tanka* (abusive words). When it comes to locks, Japanese thief jargon can spin out endless reels of inspired metaphors. There is the *ebi* (shrimp): one has to pluck and pull at the shell to break through into its delicate body; the *hana* (flower), which one can pick (*toru*); and the *eri* (collar), a witty mispronunciation of *iri* (entry). Locks can be *roku* (pulley), and lock picking *rokutsuri* (pulley fishing). Some cliques call locks *yakuban* (turning part), others *tsukimushi* (attached insects). Some gangs prefer more sensitive expressions such as *momiji* (maple leaves) and *mimochi musume* (pregnant daughter); in her delicate condition she must be handled with the softest of touches. Down south, on Osaka's streets, locks are known as *aisu* (rammable blowholes), *kudarimushi* (lower insects) or *sagarimushi* (low-down insects), and further down, in Wakayama city, thieves call locks *sanpira* and *enko*.

The most ingenious way to enter a mansion is to march brashly up the garden path. Debonair thieves who simply walk up to the main door are known as *mae* (fronts). Once on the porch, each has his own method. The *aritsuke* (ant attachers), *kogatana* (daggers), *sori* (benders), and *atetsukai* (blade users) stand in full view of the street and swiftly slip their metallic contraptions into the locks to jiggle them open. The *shippiki*-needle tests the lock's sturdiness and its make, while the *takehari* (bamboo needle) and the *gen* (bamboo teakettle handle) are used to press down the tumblers. These quick-fingered lock pickers are not above working in full view of the street. A passerby glancing into the garden would see only a tired individual hunched over, fumbling tipsily with his keys.

Front doors that succumb smoothly to the professional's touch are known as *tanka ga moroi* (the curse words are fragile).

In tougher mansions, where doors are double- and even triple-locked, the *kobuya* (gnarlers), and the *yaburi* (breakers) go to work with a hatchet. Their forceful technique is called *akebabarashi* (opening-place liquidation) or *tankahiraki* (curse-word releasing). If the stalwart door still does not yield, then a small high-powered saw, the *menoko* (child of the eye), is flicked into action. This machine is used by the *shibuita hane* (board removers) and the *kiji* (grain wooders), who will saw their way through the body of the door and leave the locked frame standing.

- *Komatta na! Akebabarashi no saichū ni ate ga dame ni natchimau to wa!*
  Damn! How could my jigger have broken right as I was working that door!
- *Tankahiraki no toki ni wa arāmu ni ki o tsukero yo!*
  Be careful of the alarm when you break down that door!
- *Kono menoko de dō yatte shigoto shiro'tte yūn da yo?*
  How the hell am I supposed to work with this saw?

Doors that are made of a robust metal, with crowbar and iron cross-beam reinforcements, are called *tanka akan'* (the curse words won't open). The only door specialists who can handle these formidable barricades are the *tsuriage* (jack screwers) and the *tenbin* (weighing scales). They do what is known as *karahiku* (pulling off the husk), in which they zero in on the hinges with drills, wrenches, and blowtorches, and lift out door and frame as a unit.

Another breed of thief prefers entering through windows. The easiest, many argue, is the bathroom window, dubbed in thief jargon as either *hachinosu* (nest of the bee) or *hachisu* (bee's nest). Few of them have locks, and if they are shut from the inside a brisk jolt with a *baita*, a metal staff whose ends have been chiseled down to a sharp point, will spring the frame open. Brigands who hinge their choice of mansion on the size and approachability of this window are classed by their peers as *haiyū* (hot-water enterers).

Some thieves prefer to target the mansion's larger porch or balcony windows. These thieves travel light, their tool bags sporting a simple rope to climb to the balcony and a small diamond glass cutter to remove window panes. The jargon calls these masters *sugarahazushi*, *sugara* being the secretive reversal of *garasu* (glass), while *hazushi* means "remover." More obscurely they are *murakumo* (cloud masses).

When doors are obstructed and windows barred, the *amakiri* (heaven cutters) spring into action. Using wrenches, electric saws, or even concrete blasters, they cut, kick, saw, or boost their way through the roof. The police call these thieves *yanetsutai* (roof enterers) and *hai* (scramblers), but the men and women who brave the slippery tiles and shaky corrugated roofings give each other more elevated names. The younger ones are the *nyanzoku* (meow gang), known also more morbidly as the *nennen kozō* (sleep sleep little boy); they hope to tiptoe soundlessly through the children's room upstairs without startling an infant. Older professionals prefer the even more macabre *sagarigumo* (descending spider). They hook their ropes to the frame of the skylight and silently glide down into the house. The roof robbers define their descent into the upper rooms as *ten kara yuku* (coming from heaven). The idea of combining the heavens with burglary caught on, and soon roof specialists were inventing one grandiloquent name after another: *tenzutai* (enterers from heaven), *tengaishi* (heavenly-canopy masters), *tenshi* (heaven masters), and *tengari* and *tongari* (heaven hunters). Other names that have been passed down from generation to generation are *watarikomi* (cross-and-enterer), *neyahaguri* (roof ripper), *tatsu* (dragon), *nezumimekuri* (ripping mice), and *kamisori* ("razorblades," or looters who cut into the roof). The brand of roof thief who works exclusively at night is the *goishita* (dark down). Men and women who access roofs by shimmying up telephone poles call themselves *denshin* (telegrams) and *denshinkasegi* (telegram breadwinners). Tokyo's Chinese jargon circles donated their own mellifluous word, *teiauchintsu*.

- *Aitsu wa tengaishi dakara, doa no akekata wa shiranē yo.*
  He's a roof specialist, so he has no idea about opening doors.
- *Ano goishita-tachi wa kanojo no ie de nusumeru mono wa minna nusunjimatta yō da.*
  Those night thieves just emptied her house.
- *Aitsu watarikomi no kuse ni ochite ashi o otta rashii ze.*
  Although he's a roof specialist, he fell and broke his leg.
- *Teiauchintsu ni wa aitsu wa chitto futorisugi da ze. Dō yatte nobore'tte yūn da yo?*
  He's too fat for a telephone pole specialist. How the hell is he gonna climb up there?

Older thieves and those who prefer to keep both feet firmly on the ground specialize in what ethnic Chinese gangsters call *ryahiyatan* (swatting insects on the wall). They use a pick or sledgehammer to swat their way through the wall. In plain street-Japanese this is known as *beka o barashikamaru*, "disposing of the wall in order to crawl in" (*beka* is an inversion of *kabe*, "wall"). In some circles, wall breaking is also known as *beka naseru* (doing the wall), *beka tsukeru* (fixing the wall), and *mado ga mieru* ("the window is visible," because a hole has just been blasted into the wall). The racket of the hammering triggered the expression *mimibarashi* (tearing off the ears). Some gangsters maintain that the burglar's ears are being torn off, others that it is the mansion's, in that the building's main structure is its head, the windows its eyes, and the smashed walls its ears.

In the wild sixties and seventies wall breaking came to be called, dramatically, *harakiri*. The image was that of modern wall breakers plunging their drills and chainsaws into the soft belly of a home, much as elegant classical heroes and heroines turned noble daggers on themselves. The generation of the eighties, a more internationalized set of thieves, upgraded the *harakiri* idea with a twist of English. The most fashionable name for wall breaker, they decided, was to be *beriishi* (belly master).

If doors, locks, windows, and roof tiles prove too formidable for a pack of thieves, they solemnly declare the case to be *yawai*, ornery (from *yabai*, "dangerous"), and turn on their heels and march out of the garden. In a more unfortunate scenario, in which a light suddenly goes on in response to the sound of walls being pulverized or glass being shattered, the robbers will gasp the classical jargon term *wakatono* (young lord, i.e. "drat, someone is in after all") and make a dash for the gate.

When the robbers are in the mansion the job officially begins. The period stretching from the criminals' arrival to their loot-laden departure is called *yama* (mountain). This delicate metaphor suggests that the thieves, like pilgrims climbing mountains to reach blessed shrines, have to first drudge their way up the steep slope of breaking and entering before they can snatch the spoils from the peak. A younger synonym for the high-charged stealing period, used by trendy burglar novices in Tokyo and Osaka, is *ingu*. This strange term that leaves older criminals baffled, is none other than the English gerundive suffix "ing."

"We lifted it from English words like *dūingu* (doing), *suchiiruingu* (stealing), *robbingu* (robbing)," the youngsters explain.

- *Yama no saichū ni mono oto o taterun ja nē zo!*
  Don't make a sound while we're on the job!
- *Oi yabē, isoge yo! Yama ni sanjippun ijō kakeru mon ja nē ze!*
  Shit, man, move it! We shouldn't be on the job more than thirty minutes!
- *Shh! Ingu no saichū ni shaberun ja nē!*
  Shh! Don't talk on the job!
- *Ingu no saichū ni nanka warui yokan ga shiyagaru.*
  I've been having a bad feeling about this job since we started it.

As the burglars move to the "mountain" portion of their crime, they will perform *atari*, the very last precautionary check before their feet hit the mansion's polished parquet. If all is well, they will plunge like swords into the inner sanctum of the home, the *yasa* (from *saya*, "sheath"). With their flashlights they sneak from room to room searching for loot. This is opaquely described as *miagari sashite miru* (our bodies are moving up in search of). On this initial round nothing is touched. The aim is to "bite the platform" (*dai o kamu*), to flavor the spoils, mentally balancing their portability against their potential market value. "If we had to choose, should we take the TV-video set, the CD player with remote, or that gigantic Kamakura vase?" the bandits ask themselves. Another burning question is whether the articles being considered are *abuiabu* (the real thing). When thieves come across prospective bounty that is of contestable value, the connoisseur of the group does a quick *atari o tsukeru* (attaching a hit). He or she will carefully scratch, bite, lick, or prod the item to test its authenticity. A thief who bumps into an expensive object and sends it crashing to the floor, is accused of *buriya*, the jargon word for smashing stealable commodities on the job.

- *Chikushō! Koko ni wa nani hitotsu abuiabu ga ari'ya shinē!*
  Shit! Absolutely nothing here's genuine!
- *Oi, kore ga honmono ka chitto atari tsukete miru beki da ze.*
  Hey, check this piece to see if it's real.
- *Aitsu o tsurete ikun' dattara, burya ni ki o tsuketa hō ga ii ze!*
  If you're gonna take him along, make sure he doesn't trash the place!

Some modern looters are only interested in hard yen. Unperturbed, they will march right past rich bibelots and strings of Picassos and make a beeline for the safe, for what they call *mamono* (the real thing). These looters are the *shimabarashi* (island breakers), *otomodachi* (friends), *namashi* (cash masters), *sannokōkan* (money exchangers), and more recently *maniishi* (money masters). In money-master jargon the safe is *musume*, the daughter. A safe, like a cherished daughter, they explain, is a household's most prized and jealously-guarded possession. If the safe turns out not to have been worth cracking, the dispirited specialists mutter *musume ga wakai* (their daughter is young). If, on the other hand, yen notes come pouring out, the joyous proclamation is *musume ga haramu* (their daughter is with child).

The exhilarating moment when a looter hits the jackpot is known as *makenshi*. This argot word describes the rushing of blood to one's head, the gasp of exhilaration, the joyful stagger. When money is found in an unexpected place, the expressions used are *morai* (receiving) and *ogami* (prayer—the surprised thief kneels in thankful prayer).

- *Yā, maitta, maitta! Kongetsu haitta ie wa zenbu musume ga wakakatta ze!*
  Man, this sucks! All the houses we did this month had safes that were slim pickings!
- *Aitsu no me ni kakar'ya musume ga haranderu ka dōka nante ippatsu de wakatchimau ze.*
  That guy, man! One glance at a safe and he knows if it's full!
- *Nijippun-kan sagashite, yatto makenshi to kita!*
  We searched for twenty minutes, and then bull's eye!
- *Kono e no ura nijūman mo mitsukeru nante tonda morai da ze!*
  Man, the jackpot behind this picture! Two hundred thousand yen!

After the thieves finish exploring the premises the actual thieving begins. The intense phase in which money, jewelry, portable antiques, and objets d'art are raked into sacks is known as *hayakoto* (the quick thing). After *hayakoto*, thieves with nerves of steel dart into the kitchen for a quick snack, a habit classified in jargon as *hantebiki* (food snatching).

Once the plunder sacks are tied shut, the word to hiss is the Korean *aruikara* (the loot is assembled). If the goods are exceptionally rich, the looters will add *kanchira*, Japanese Korean for "the catch was good." In unpolished circles, the bandits will cap the burglary with what some call *ki ga fuseru* (plopping down the spirit), others *higa barasu* (rubbing out the misdeed). One of the group hobbles to the door, yanks his trousers down, and crouching, defecates. This tasteless action, burglars explain, is the only surefire method of duping police dogs. One whiff and the animal is totally disoriented.

- *Kondo no ki ga fuseru no ban wa dare da?*
  Who's turn is it to shit by the door?
- *Mata higa barashita! Mattaku aitsu wa!*
  Don't tell me he took a shit again! I really wish he wouldn't!
- *Higa barashi ni itta, omē kitanē yatsu da na!*
  You took a shit by the door? You're sick!

The final dash for the door is referred to as *ketsubaru* (stretching one's ass). Thieves leaving the premises with sacks swung over their shoulders are doing *saya kaeri* (changing the sheath).

The gang scuttles into the yard, over the wall and out the gate, scattering in all directions. This is *mochizura* (having and running). To leave the scene of the crime in a congenial group would be suicidal; the only safe thing to do is what Tokyo's Koreans call *chacha*: each member dashes down a different alley. Groups of burglars who only steal money and jewelry will often do *chōyapabataro*; the loot is passed to one person to reduce the danger of the whole group being rounded up by the police. In some of the rougher clans, however, bandits will react gingerly to the idea of entrusting their hard-earned spoils to a colleague. What if he should be *zaruo* (sieve), a loot carrier who is not above straining small valuables or yen notes out of the sack? This ignoble genre of betrayal is known among gangsters as *baiharu* (stretching the purchases) and *baigiri* (cutting the purchases).

- *Oi, shitteta ka? Zaruo ga kawa de shitai de mitsukatta ze!*
  Hey, did you know they found that sieve dead in the river?
- *Koitsu wa hen da nā! Aitsu wa baigiri shiagatta nā.*
  Something's fucked up here! I'm sure he skimmed off some of the loot.
- *Aitsu baiharu shiagatte, kondo attara bukkuroshite yaru ze!*
  That guy riffled the loot. When I run into him, I'm gonna fuckin' kill him!

In a larger clan, where loot carriers are tried and trusted, the thieves will make their way one by one back to the *shima* (island), the gang's territory. There they will re-congregate to receive their share of the booty, their *kabu* (stocks). The emotion-laden distribution of the pillage is dubbed by some gangs *kabuwari* (stock splitting), *kabuwake* (stock dividing) and *tezuke* (depositing), and by others *yamawake* (mountain splitting), *yamakan* (mountain sectioning), and *hajiki* (springing open). The thieves are on tenterhooks, and eager argotic questions abound:

- *Yoroku?* (profits)
  Was this a successful stint?
- *Rachi?* (picket fence)
  What are the results?
- *Musuko wakakatta?* (was the son young)
  There was no money in the house?
- *Yabakatta?* or *yabakaita?* (from *yabai*, "dangerous")
  Has the job been a flop?
- *Amerikan!* (American)
  This is worthless! (American coffee, the bandits explain, is ridiculously weak. Like a stolen piece of junk, it does not do anything for one).

The joyful circumstance in which loot turns out to be of much higher value than anticipated is gaily heralded with *atsui* (it is thick). Another even cheerier occasion occurs when, during the loot dividing, an unexpectedly large wad of banknotes is found stashed in an antique or in the lining of a picture. This circumstance is dubbed *atari* (hit).

Burglars who work in twos and threes often prefer to split the loot at the scene of the crime. This way, everyone can do an immediate *dankon utsu* (bullet-hole banging), rushing off home after a successful job. This expression is always good for a raucous laugh, since *dankon utsu*, if written with the characters "male-root banging" can also mean "banging the penis." *Oi, hayaku dankon utō ze!* (Yo man, let's split!) could with a giggle be misinterpreted as "Yo man, let's bang penises!"

2 ▪ Reckless Burglars

THE CRIMINALS who live most dangerously are the *odorikomi* (those who enter dancing). Unlike their cousins the *akisunerai* (empty-nest targeters), the *odorikomi* do not check, recheck, and then check again before kicking doors in. If money is to be had, they will break and enter. Over time, the jargon of Japanese burglars playfully developed the bad boys' dancing image, and soon even the toughest thugs came to be jocularly known as *odoriko* (danseuses). The terpsichorean theme went even further, and these rash methods of burglary came to be known as *bon odori*, from the dances of Obon, the summer Festival of the Dead.

- *Ōsaka no odoriko ga mata tsukamatta ze!*
  That danseuse from Osaka was caught again!
- *Konban no bon odori umaku yare yo!*
  Good luck at tonight's dance!

The burglars enjoyed the festive idea of combining august ceremony with barging into houses, and were soon calling each other both *obon* and *urabon* (from the older Sanskrit name for the rituals, Ullambana). The

Obon festival was originally held in July, which prompted rough looters also to be called *shichigatsu* (seventh month), and then *nanoka* and *nanuka* (seventh day), which finally became the even more esoteric *ichiroku* ("one-six," i.e. seven). As more and more areas in Japan began celebrating the festival in August, some gangs simply called their tougher burglars *hachigatsu* (eighth month), while more traditional gangs stuck to the old words.

Dancing thieves live on the edge. Some have actually become specialists in entering *orusu* (occupied nests); these are the *hamahori* (beach diggers) and *nobori* (risers). While the family is eating or watching television in one room, they tiptoe from closet to closet collecting valuables. Some thieves wait until the family is safely in bed; these are the *kurumi* (walnuts). Their silent method of entry is known as *seburikameru* (sleeping crawl). Related to them are the *machi* (those who wait), the *irimachi* (those who enter and wait), and the *tomari* (those who stay over). They break into occupied houses and then hide in a closet or under a bed until the family goes out. Then the heist begins.

Hiding in an occupied house is known as *anko* (bean jam). The jam, the tough burglars explain, is always hidden inside the *anpan* (bean-jam bun), just like thieves are concealed in the house. The drawback of this style of looting is that there is a good chance of bumping into the family. The victims are liable to start "dancing" (*odoru*), jumping up and down and waving their hands in terror, often followed by what is known as *nekatsukareru*, the backwards version of *kane o tsukareru* ("hitting the gong," or screeching for help). If the burglar is lucky the family will now scuttle out of the house and make for the nearest police station, a situation referred to with the tongue-twisted Korean *teitotsuchiyotsuta*.

Some victims, however, will not run. Confronted, a rough burglar will turn into *inaori* (a stay-and-fixer). He will do *pika* (flick out a switchblade), flash his *pachinko* ("pinball machine," in this case a gun) or resort to binding and gagging. This is known as *hosokukuri* (thin knotting), *kumo ni kakeru* (being caught by the spider), and *maki ni awasu* (letting someone experience the roll). Some burglars will vent their frustration at being caught by beating up the victim in what is known as *tsunagu* (connecting). When it is a housewife who is being tied up, the brute phrase used is *yachi o jime ni kakeru* (tying up the cunt).

- *Inaori ni naru shika hōhō wa nai ze.*
  The only way to be a heistman is to be rough when you have to be.
- *Aitsu ni pachinko o tsukitsukete miro yo! Ippen de damatchimau ze!*
  Shove your gun into his face! That should shut him up!
- *Yabē! Barechimatta! Hayaku aitsu o kumo ni kakero!*
  Fuck! He's caught us! We're gonna have to tie him up quick!
- *Tsunagareta yatsu ima byōin ni iru rashii ze.*
  I hear the guy we roughed up is in the hospital now.

The roughest of the "dancing" thieves are the *tonton* (bang bang), *tonma* (bang devils), *ishiwari* (stone break-ers), *tatakizeme* (banging attack), *tataki* and *hataki* (bangers), and *sharitataki* (those who bang for profit).

As the ominous "bang" element in their names suggests, these burglars do not gasp and run when they are caught. Those who cross them end up what the ethnic Chinese call *jara* ("snipped," from *jia le*), *suichō* ("fast asleep," from *shui jiao*), or *chōra* ("broken," from *zhe le*).

Some burglars are not above barging into bedrooms to rape sleeping victims. This practice is referred to as *tsukeme* (touching eyes), an expression that, oddly enough, has some connection to Buddhist priest slang. *Tsuke* is "touching" (touching the woman), and *me*, "eyes," is the priestly euphemism for money.

The language of the toughest clans is filled with elaborate expressions for raping while on the job. One of the most common terms, *menuki* (eye pulling), carries on the priestly Buddhist practice of connecting eyes with money, but also manages to combine it with the violent image of physical torture. *Neshin* and *neshi* (sleep specialists) are the men who target bedrooms after the loot has been assembled and packed. After World War II tough sesquipedalian terms of Korean background flooded the Tokyo scene, and the Japanese bandits, in a show of solidarity with their Korean colleagues, struggled to pronounce them. The protracted Korean words *makuirebabantonda* and *hitekipuchinta* were used for rape that caps a theft, while the even lengthier *marubanichiyomendā* implies that the robbed housewife not only consented to intercourse but actually enjoyed it. On those rare occasions when a group of burglars rape a male victim, the expression used is *yārietsu*, the Japanese pronunciation of the Yokohama Chinese *yan lie zi* (lining up despicably on a young man).

When Things Go Wrong

The first sign that a criminal project might be jinxed is *awaji*, bumping into a policeman on the way to the job. Even if the officer smiles, and pleasantly tips his cap, many high-strung looters will stop in their tracks and abort the mission.

Meeting a policeman while one is kneeling in front of a gate, the picking pin lodged in the lock, is a more grievous issue. The underworld rocks with laughter at the hapless burglar so caught, and pronounces him *pikari* (flashed) and *hanbe* ("waited upon," from *hanberu*). To ward off arrest and mockery, the careful clans post sentries. At the first sign of a patrol car or a uniformed officer these men and women will hiss one of the many thief words for cop: *bōfuri!* (stick swinger), *surikogi!* (wooden pestle), *enma!* (devil), *hige!* (beard), *hoshi!* (star), *kā-sama!* (mommy), *udonya!* (noodle vendor) or, on a lighter note, *pii-chan!* (little Mr. P). On hearing these warning words thieves will cram their widgets and jiggers into their tool bags and run.

The secret words for "cop!" can save lives at every stage, and gangs throughout Japan glut and re-glut their vocabularies with synonyms and metaphors. Foreigners often marvel at the abundance of animal imagery: policemen can be *aobuta* (blue pigs), *en* (monkeys), *etekō* (apes), *karasu* (crows), *aokarasu* (blue crows), *itachi* (weasels), *ahiru* (ducks) *hayabusa* (falcons), *ahōdori* ("idiotic birds," or albatrosses), *kē* ("dogs," from the Korean *kae*), *barori* (Korean for pig), and *koyani* ("cat," from the Korean *koyangi*). Officers even turn into insects such as *hachi* (bees), *dani* (ticks), *kumo* (spiders), *mushi* (bugs), and *kejirami* (pubic lice).

There is more to the unusually large number of Japanese street words for police than just the burglars' fevered linguistic imaginations. The code words often carry with them reams of useful information. Is the policeman armed? Is he in a car? Does he look aggressive? Is the gang a match for him? *Inta!* for instance, means "Careful, there's an officer patrolling the neighborhood!" *Pākā!* stands for, "Patrol car! Run for your life!" Equally alarming is *gokiburi* (cockroach). The policeman in this case is on a motorcycle, and can follow the burglars over pavements and through parks. *Kijirushi* (devil's mark) implies that a whole mobile unit is arriving and there is no point in running. The looters are cornered, and might as well line up on the pavement with their hands up.

The secret words can also tell us about the policeman's character and disposition. *Yaba* (from *yabai*, "dangerous") is a tough, fierce-looking officer, while *wankō* (woof woof) is the type who looks hot-tempered and irritable. *Oji* (uncle) is a dangerous middle-aged patrolman who knows all the members of the gang by name and is liable to blow the whistle first and ask questions later. *Kazaguruma* (windmill) is an officer who circles the streets and alleys, getting closer and closer to the area where the criminals are working. The most dangerous are *oyahine* (daddy gnarl), *oyadama* (daddy bullet), and *ōbune* (ocean liner), who are all chief inspectors. If these august men appear in person, then one of the gang must be *aori* (stimulator), an undercover agent, or worse, *aka-chan* (little Mr. Red), an informer, and the criminals' stealing days are over.

Other coded warnings are of a happier nature. *Aokuri* means, "It's only a traffic cop, act natural."

Daikon megane (radish with glasses) means, "Relax, the officer is new and an obvious hick." *Akapori* (red police), *hime* (princess), *poriman* (a contraction of "police" and "woman"), and *suke* (bitch) herald the arrival of a female officer or officers. The sexist undertone of this language is, "Don't worry, it's just a woman."

Ethnic Korean and Chinese words for police are especially popular among Japanese burglars. The words are tough, they are exotic, and probably unknown to the all-Japanese police force. Tokyo's Korean words, like *kumōgi*, *komucha*, and *chonbu*, imply that the policeman is in uniform, while the Yokohama jargon gives plainclothesmen names of Chinese background like *tsuai*, *rinhatsu*, *tamu*, and *oa*.

- *Konna kumōgi bakkari ga iru tokoro e hairo nante—omae ki demo kuruttan ja nē no ka?*
  You're not gonna break into a place full of cops? Are you nuts?
- *Kinō sakaba de tonari ni suwatteta yatsu komucha dattan da'tte yo! Omae shinjirareru ka?*
  The guy next to us at the bar was a cop! Can you believe that?
- *Yā! Asetta yo! Ore-tachi ga chōdo niwa e shinobikonda toki chonbu ga yoko o sudōri shitan da yo!*
  Man, I freaked! We'd just crawled into the garden when a cop walked right by!
- *Mattaku hidoi mon da ze! Kono hen wa ima tamu ga uyo uyo shiterun da ze.*
  It's a disaster! The whole neighborhood is full of cops!
- *Oi, yabe! Oa ga kita zo! Hayaku, zurakarō ze!*
  Shit! The cops are here! Quick, let's split!

While looters are engaged in pillage, their nerves are on edge. The tremulous *kamisori?* (razor blade?) or *kamisori shinai ka?* (isn't it doing razor blade?) are questions of Korean background meaning, "Footsteps?" and "Do I hear footsteps?"

If the footsteps become louder, the panicking gangsters will wail *kaminari ochiru* ("thunder is falling," meaning, "Shit! A police raid!"), an expression swiped from Tokyo's illegal gambling circles. The looters will rush to the window to check the street. If they see their lookout standing handcuffed by the gate, and patrol cars converging, they are likely to groan *ami o haru* (they are stretching a net), meaning that the law has surrounded the building. As always at times of great stress, the robbers resort to heavy jargon:

- *Tetsuta!* (of Korean origin)
  Look over there! The police have arrived!
- *Dotsutā!* (of Korean origin)
  The police are here!
- *Iei!* (Tokyo jargon)
  Help! Danger! SOS!
- *Nashiware!* (an inversion of *shina*, "goods," and *ware*, "broken")
  We're ruined! They've found us out!
- *Nashihare!* (an inversion of "goods" and *hareru*, "become clear")
  We've been found out!
- *Ketsu o watta!* (the ass was cleaved)
  We must have fucked up somewhere!
- *Isu o sasatta!* (the chair was wedged)
  We've been informed on!
- *Yabu no naka de he o hita!* (somebody farted in the bush)

One of us here is a traitor!
- *Ushi no tsume!* (cow's nails)
  The police was in on the deal from the start!
- *Tējitari!* ("pork chops," of Korean origin)
  Get out your guns!
- *Tsue o motte!* (hold the stick)
  We have to get our act together now and really keep our eyes peeled!
- *Michi ga warui!* (the road is bad)
  The police are everywhere! It doesn't look like we'll get out!
- *Ore-tachi yukiya no usagi!* (we're rabbits in a snow house)
  Our situation is pretty precarious!
- *Kama o tsukō!* (let's pound a pot, with "pot" meaning "ass")
  Everyone, hide!
- *Gesozure!* (rub your tentacles)
  Run!
- *Mau!* (dance)
  Flee!
- *Rāhowa!* ("pluck flowers," in Chinese gang jargon)
  Make a dash for it!

In the growing din of sirens, barking police dogs, smashing glass, and officers storming the place, the burglars are facing fiasco. The staunch Korean word they use to sum up this desperate situation is *barumburotsuta* (the wind has blown). Cornered, the criminals must now seek out what is known as *ana* (a hole)—a metaphorical hole, which will save the gang from the mortal danger. The leader of the pack might give a short emergency speech in which he urges his fellow looters to face the calamity with as much sang-froid as they can muster. He might also quote a few well-chosen crab proverbs to prove his point:

- *Urotae kani ana ni irazu.*
  A flustered crab will miss its hole.
- *Kani wa kōra ni nisete ana o horu.*
  The crab will dig a hole that fits its shell.
  (Each looter should use his wit and cunning to escape).

The worst scenario is classified as *daimaki*, also pronounced *taimaki* (platform rolling). The thieves are arrested in the home they are looting, holding the *sanyabukuro* or *chanshiki*, the tool bags, in one hand, and a stolen item or two in the other. The general idea is that if one is to be arrested one should have a minimum number of incriminating objects on one's person. The governing proverb advises, *He o koite, shiri o subete* (You farted, now close your ass). Although one has broken the law (by farting) one can still get rid of the evidence (and pretend nothing happened).

One way to do this is *uraita* (ceiling), to hide the loot in a safe place. The bandits can always do *donden* (topsy-turvy), return to the scene of the crime at a safer date. If the situation is *isogashii* (busy), meaning that the criminals are running down the street with the police at their heels, more desperate measures are called for. If their loot is ballasting them down, they must *enzuke* (marry it off), the desperate euphemism for ditching the plunder. Clever burglars will drop their loot piecemeal, in the hope that they will have something left when they get home. This is known as *gan, kan, ganta*, and *kanta*.

If the police start gaining on the fleeing burglars, the burglars' favorite term is the vivacious Chinese expression *shanrai shunrai* (from *shang lai*, "it's coming up," and *shui lai*, "the water is coming"). With the floodwater lapping at their feet the sweating crooks will fling their expensive burglar tools in all directions. This is known as *hake* (sweeping) and *chari furu* (swinging the clinks).

Some of the thief's most poignant words are reserved for the stirring moment of his arrest. The criminals describe themselves as *kuzureru* (collapsing), *hikkakeru* (being hooked), *nejiru* (being wrenched), *nukaru* (bungling), and *anberu* (Nagasaki slang for "being punched"). The policemen whip out the handcuffs: the *wappa* (rings), *chin* (clonks), *kai* (shells), *shaka-sama* (Lord Buddhas), or *kakushi* (that which is covered), and the bandits, so as not to lose face in front of the gaping crowd, are allowed to cover the cuffs with a jacket or a scarf.

But all is not yet lost. Bandits worth their mettle will try to perform *tachikorobi* (a standing tumble), overpowering the police in the van. Then everyone rolls out into the street and to freedom.

3 ▪ Picking Pockets in Tokyo

THE MOST colorful group of Japanese thieves is made up of little clusters of small-time professionals. These are the *suri* (those who rub up against), *hittakuri* (snatch and handlers), *tsukami* (grippers), *kakekomi* (those who dash into places), and *kakedashi* (those who dash out of places). They weave through crowds, riffling pockets and bags, wallets and briefcases, snatching money at market counters, movie theaters, in dark sex booths, and in train stations, from the masses on rush-hour trains, buses, ferry boats, and inter-island ships. The *ato oshi* (rear pushers) will jostle their victims from behind: a brisk shove, followed by a *sumimasen, shitsurei itashimashita* (oh, excuse me, I'm so sorry), and the wallet is gone. The *muneate* (chest aimers) and *nakasashi* (inside inserters) work on the Tokyo subway, sliding their hands into the breast pockets of expensive business suits. The *seoimaki* (burden relievers) lift valuables out of tourists' heavy backpacks. The *kanizukai* (crab users), *tsumi* (snippers), and *kamisori ma* (razor devils) incise their way into deep coat pockets and leather handbags. These men and women go to work with custom-made blades and tweezers which are known in back-alley slang as *take no fue* (bamboo whistles), *kane* (metal), *bakakiri* (idiot cutters), and *takegushi* (bamboo skewers). A younger set, the *kurumaoi* (car chasers) and the *kurumaoshi* (car pushers), make a living by motorcycling past rows of cars during rush hour traffic, leaning into open windows and snatching jewelry, handbags, and briefcases.

There are even groups who work exclusively in temples. These are the *miyashi* (shrine specialists), *yamabushi* (hermits), and *kanesu* (from *kane suri*, "bell pickpockets"). Dodging the sharp eye of the watchful clergy, they collect ornate golden hairpins from women kneeling in kimono, swipe yen notes tucked tightly into festive *obi* belts, filch the money that the devout throw at the statue of the Buddha, and then rake through the holy donation boxes.

In the tough hierarchy of Japan's criminal classes these quiet, unostentatious pilferers are ranked rock bottom. Star gangsters call them fly chasers (*haeoi*) and branch rippers (*eda hagi*), a pungent expression that meant "panty thief" during the desperate post-World War II years, when suburban women were in the habit of hanging their expensive undergarments on tree branches. After a few drinks at the sake bar, and a few karaoke songs, the elitist criminals find even unkinder names for these minor-league lawbreakers: *chibo* and *bochi*, *chibi* and *bichi*, *chiko*, *chiki*, *chikiya*, and *yakichi*, all discriminatory dialect words for "dwarf." The Lilliputian reasoning is that pickpockets move through crowds almost as if stumbling between their victim's legs. After a few more drinks, the criminal elite call the pickpockets on trains *uke* (receivers), a malevolent word for vagina, while thieves on ferry boats become *bōdō,* an equally malevolent word for penis.

- *Odoroita nā! Kono tōri zentai wa haeoi darake da ze!*
  Man! This whole place is just full of little jostlers!
- *Aitsu jibun o nani-sama da to omotte yagarun da? Taka ga eda hagi da ze.*
  Who the fuck does he think he is? He's no more than a two-bit panty thief.
- *Mattaku odoroita kott'a! Satsu wa imada ni ano bochi o tsukamae nanrenēn da ze.*
  I'm just real surprised that frisker hasn't been caught by the police yet.
- *Aitsu wa tada no uke da ze! Hajiki no tsukaikata nante shitteru wake nē daro!*
  He's just a little train thief! He wouldn't know how to use a gun!
- *Ferii de minato ni tsuita toki, bōdō o mita ze.*
  Just as we were arriving in the port on the ferry, I saw this prick working the crowd.

The wallet heisters and crowd jostlers, spurned by the big-time clans of the inner city, ganged together to create small leagues and corporations of their own. To accentuate their autonomy and ward off prying ears, they vigorously nurtured and expanded their private lingoes. Words were invented for every type of pocket, for the pockets' position in a garment, the material of the lining, the hand movement into the pocket, and the hand movement out of the pocket. New verbs were created to cover the most Byzantine stealing techniques. *Nakanuku* (inside pull-out), for instance, means "to carefully slip one's hand into a victim's trouser pocket, draw out the wallet, flick it open, whip out cash and credit cards, close it, and slip it back into the victim's trouser pocket." *Hikobarasu* covers the same procedure with a twist; the wallet is not in the trouser pocket but in the inside coat pocket. An even fiercer verb, *takudasu* (kindle and pull out), means "to drop, as if by mistake, a lit cigarette into a victim's jacket or open shirt, and then, while the victim is frantically trying to locate the burning butt, come to his aid, helping him unbutton and frisk through jacket, shirt, and undershirt, taking the opportunity to lift wallets and other valuables out of pockets and bags."

Another pivotal jargon verb, *maitobasu* (dance and fly), means to walk towards a rich-looking victim, spot the bulging wallet in his trousers, and with a masterful snap of the hand whisk it out as the victim passes. As more and more Tokyo gangs adopted this technique, it appeared in different parts of town as *mondorikiru* (somersault cut), *chigai o mau* (dancing in contrast), *chigai o matsuru* (celebrating in contrast), and *chigai o kau* (shopping in contrast), along with popular shortened varieties such as *chigai* (contrast), and its inversion *gaichi*.

The clans grew and split and grew again, and the jargon of petty theft became richer and richer. Pickpockets could now rattle off scores of secret words for wallet: *hōza, nakasuki, umo, tai, yū, jinsuke, yoite, bochi, zuda, yoichi* and *yoichibē, chinkichi* and *jinkichi*. Some gangs named their wallets *nasu* (eggplants), *iwa* (rocks), *kaeru* (frogs), *kaerudachi* (frogs' friends), *ike* (buried), and *pāsu* (the English word "purse"); other gangs went for more inspired expressions like *hitsujiire* (sheep entrance). A sheep, they explain, will readily eat paper, and paper is used to make money, and money goes into wallets . . . so why not call a wallet a sheep entrance? Subtler expressions like *rokkupu* and *miire* refer specifically to the money inside the wallet, while *ike* ("buried," as in buried treasure) is used exclusively when a wallet divulges an electrifyingly large wad of notes. Some provincial gangs, however, will use *ike* to mean "wallet," their reasoning being that wallets are buried in trouser pockets.

If a wallet proves to be empty, the verdict is *mosagara* (from *mosa kara*, "the gut is empty") or *iwagara* (from *iwa kara*, "the stone is empty").

Outsiders listening in on this charismatic jargon will hear eccentric statements such as:

- *Aitsu wa shin'iri dakara, mada chigai o mau koto wa dekinē yo.*

  He's new, so he still can't dance in contrast.
- *Nan'te kott'a! Chigai o matsutteru saichū ni kuso-nasu otosh'chimatta ze!*

  Man, I tell you! Right in the middle of celebrating in contrast, I dropped the fucking eggplant!
- *Tsuite nē nā! Kyō no iwa wa doremo hotondo kara data ze!*

  No luck, man! Today's rocks were almost all empty!
- *Kono hitsujiire ni wa ikura haiterun da ze? Chotto hayaku mite miro yo!*

  How much is in the sheep entrance? Quick, take a look!

Foreigners who spend time lurking around urban train stations are likely to be amazed at the change in the jargon's lilt as they stray from one clan's territory into the next. On the Chiyoda-ku side of Tokyo station, for instance, they might hear *nakaba* and *nakabba* for "inside pocket," while a few hundred yards away on the Chuo-kú side, the pocket might turn into a more plosive *nakapa*. If they were to wander a mile or so in the direction of the port, the pocket changes into *uchiba* (inside place) and, on the waterfront, first into *chippa*, and then by the waterbus terminal into *hikopa*.

Working the Crowd

When pickpockets work in groups they describe themselves as *yama o kumu* (gathering into a mountain). They form clans, with leaders, bag specialists and wallet specialists, and sometimes loot carriers, loot concealers, diversion creators, and lookouts. If they are the kind of group that enjoys working crowds, then Tokyo pickpocketese refers to them as *batazoku* (clamor gangs), *hirabazoku* (wide place gangs), and *mogurizoku* (dividing gangs). One or two members will push and jostle their way through the masses collecting bags and wallets, which they then pass to colleagues who are known as *tatemai* (framework) and *daitsukimono* (the person who sticks to the base). These are well-dressed individuals, usually with an adamantine pillar-of-society look about them, who trail at a safe distance carrying all the wallets and bags. If there is a police bust they sidle off with the goods, and the pickpocket remains loot-free and innocent. This technique of stealing and passing is known as *matsu*, from *matsubazue* (crutches).

In some clans the thieves will split up and work the crowd from different angles. They are called *yaritemai*, and use basic no-frills pickpocketing techniques such as *okihiki* (put and pull) and *narabihiki* (move parallel with and pull). They walk or stand next to the pedestrian, hoist the wallet, and then do *dakko*, the flicking movement of the palm that will send the goods up into the sleeve. When sleeves are full, wallets and bank notes are flushed out and passed to the loot carriers.

In larger clans, pickpockets split into sets of two to increase their volume. These twosomes are given avian names such as *oshidori* (mandarin duck), and *basa* (flutter). A popular duo trick is *sotomo* (outer face), in which one partner stumbles into the victim, bows and apologizes, while the other partner cleans out pockets and bags. In a denser crowd, the couple might go for a simpler *maku o haru* (spreading the curtain). The idea here is to stand so close to one's victim that one's partner's working hand is completely hidden from view. A related method is the dramatic *maku o kiru*, a theater expression meaning to raise the curtain or start the performance. The curtain, in this case, is a magazine or a newspaper which is raised quickly and opportunely to cover the victim's face. The performance lasts a few seconds, the curtain comes down, and the players scuttle off with their loot.

- *Koko de okihiki, asoko de narabihiki—kore wa boro mōke da ze!*
  A little riffle here, a little dip there—you can make a killing!
- *Nanda omae! Semai sode ja dakko ni naranē ze!*
  C'mon man! That sleeve's too tight. How d'you expect to slip things up there?

- *Aitsu wa ate ni naranē kara, oshidori yaru no wa gomen da ze!*
  He's just totally unreliable, there's no way I'd partner up with him!
- *Ore wa matsu nuki ja shigoto wa shinē yo! Baka yū na yo!*
  I'd never work unless I had someone to pass the loot to! Don't talk shit!

The man in charge of the group is called by some *kiku* (criterion), by others less sophisticated, *gyūji* (cow's ear). In the largest operations, he will sit in a high-rise office with a view, and marshal operatives by phone, beeper, or computer e-mail, but in smaller enterprises he will be out there, his hands slipping in and out of pockets. Whether working in absentia or on location, his vital function is to be the group's referee. He will call the players together, set the strategy, signal the start, and, when the game is over, flag the players off the field. To secure the safety of his operatives he employs lookouts to eye street entrances and exits for possible patrols. These are the *katobu* (mosquito is flying), *tsuki* (attached), *torisu* and *sutori*, both inverted versions of *suri to* (with the pickpocket). Groups that have Korean underworld connections call their lookouts by the ultra-secret Korean code names *kunni* and *chiye*. In the event of a botched job these lookouts double as lifesaving buffers and stumbling blocks. As the screaming victims run after the pickpockets the lookouts, masquerading as concerned bystanders or curious onlookers, can skitter into the way, blocking, tripping, or even tackling the victims if need be.

At the Station

Many talented pickpockets work in train stations. These are taxi-stand jostlers, ticket-line heisters, waiting-room prowlers, many brands of train-riding thief, and platform pros. All have their own federations, distinct working methods, and own special blend of station pickpocketese known as *shaba ago* (from *teishaba*, "railroad depot," and *ago*, "jaw").

When a train pulls in everyone jumps to attention. The platform specialists are the first on the scene. They are the *giri* ("grabbers," from *nigiru*, "to grab"), *girijin* (grab men), *giriya* (grab dealers), *girisha* (grab individuals), *girishi* (grab specialists), and *girikonosha* (grab-guy individuals). Some platform prowlers prefer the tough ethnic Korean word *parami* (wind). Like a strong gust, the reasoning goes, they sweep over platforms, taking with them wallets, bags, briefcases, and even pieces of luggage.

- *Dō yū wake ka getsuyō wa giri ga ōin da yo na.*
  For some reason the place is teeming with grabbers every Monday.
- *Kyō wa hoka no girijin wa doko ni itchimattan dai?*
  Where did all the grab men go today?
- *Densha ga okureteru kara parami no renchū wa cha demo nomi ni itten ja nē ka.*
  The train's late, so I guess all the winds are off drinking tea.

The train doors open, and there is a stampede of passengers shuffling and jostling their way to the exits. The waiting criminals call this situation *ori* (from *oriru*, "to descend"). In the five or ten minutes until the platform is empty again there is a stealing frenzy known as *oritsukai* (using the descent) and *utsu* (to hit). Each pro has his own methods: some go for simple pocketpicking, known as *shakuru*, others steal bags, *bankakai* (the backwards version of *kabankai*, "bag shopping"). Other platform specialists do *hineri, butsu,* and *butsuri,* snipping off golden chains and necklaces, and still others thread through the throng clutching what platform jargon calls *geshihaku,* a small dagger-like contraption. These thieves do *oitore:* walking next to a well dressed victim, they plunge the razor-sharp instrument into his fancy attaché case, cut the side open, and hope to hit the jackpot.

The careful platform pro, however, will stand back and watch the passengers alight from the train. His sixth sense tells him who is the perfect victim or *hakoagari* (box descender), and on seeing him will immediately barge his way through the crowd. This stalking of victims on platforms is known as *horōi.*

As the crowd begins to disperse, a second group of thieves jumps into action. These are the *hakonori* (box riders), *hakotsukai* (box users), *hakoshi* (box specialists), *nagabakoshi* (long-box specialists), *kanebakoshi* (money-box specialists), and *hakogayoi* (box transcenders). They spot the well-dressed victims on the platform and follow them onto the train. In Japanese criminal jargon the train is always treated as a box. *Hako* (box) and its backward version *koha, kanebako* (money box), *nagabako* (long box), *gomibako* (trash can), and among older criminal riders even *shamisen,* the traditional box-like string instrument.

Victims come in all shapes. The *nemu, gaisha* (from

higaisha, "victim"), and *dōroku* (road number six) are the easiest marks. They are obviously not Tokyoites; they brandish their wallets, count their yen notes in full view of the platform sharks, and leave briefcases and luggage leaning against a stanchion while they go shopping for last-minute snacks. The drawback is that this type of prey does not usually carry anything worth stealing. One niche up is the victim who at first glance looks provincial and not worth robbing, but on closer scrutiny shows definite signs of hidden wealth. Pickpockets give this type of passenger the ethnic Korean name *poniwata*. Another eligible victim is characterized as *honkai* (true purchase) and *honke* (true home); a clear outline of the bulging wallet in a trouser pocket can be seen from a distance. The best victims are *nukui* (warm), *namahaku* (cash vomiters), and *norikin* (riding gold). Lost, confused, and provincial, they stand on platforms blinking at the electronic arrival and departure screens, big wads of yen notes practically falling out of their pockets.

- *Asoko ni tatteru gaisha o neratte miru ka?*
  Shall we go for that easy mark standing over there?
- *Aitsu wa mikake wa ā da ga, poniwata ni chigainē!*
  That guy looks like shit, but he's definitely loaded!
- *Oi, miro yo! Ano honkai nogasu beki ja nē ze.*
  Yo! Don't let that true purchase get away!
- *Yā! Maita nāa! Koryā! Mare ni miru norikin da ze!*
  Ooh, man, yeaaah! That guy there's a rare riding gold.

The final minutes before the train pulls out of the station are charged with fervid anticipation. The train jostler's nimble eye glazes as he culls and reculls all the eligible victims, hastily weighing the pros and cons of following them onto the train. The victim that he finally places his faith in is called *toku* (the beneficial one).

The final announcements roll over the loudspeaker. The warning sounds, the doors are about to close, and passengers bustle on the platform. The thief's heart begins to flutter.

- *Oi! Tanomu kara! Kono densha ni notte kure yo nā, toku-san yō!*
  Oh please, please! Please ride this train, Mr. Beneficial One!

The glorious moment in which the victim picks up bags and briefcases and steps onto the train is designated in platform jargon as *iwai* (celebration). Relieved, the happy thief climbs on board and the electronic doors close behind him.

The platform pros are not the only thieves to run for the train. The *okinagashi* (those who put and flow) climb on a local at one station, grab bags and coats, cameras and camcorders, and then jump off at the following station. In the meantime, the *tanashi* (shelf specialists) clean out the racks above the seats, while the *bataoi*, *minzō*, *bega*, *suka*, and *gyūta* steer clear of bags and cases, and go picking from pocket to pocket. When thieves meet colleagues on trains they cordially avoid each other's turf, and the cars are carefully split into thievery arenas. Those nearest the engine are the *maeba* (the front place—a sprightly pun on *maeba*, "front teeth"), the next few cars are the *ueba* (upper place, or "upper teeth"), and the last several cars the *atoba* (after place).

In train jargon pockets are known as *pā*. As the thief moves smiling from passenger to passenger, his first task is to spot the wallet or, if that does not work, fall back on his thievish instinct. If that does not work either, he will do *momiwake* (grope and understand), also known more nefariously as *sagari ni kiku* (listening down there), in which fingers run lightly over and about the creases of the victim's trousers. Oddly enough, this is also referred to as *kenjiru* (to make an offering), and *ogamu* (to pray).

- *Saifu o suru mai ni wa dono pā mo momiwake shinakucha na!*
  I had to feel up all the pockets before I got my hands on the wallet!
- *Ima wa renchū minna haba no hiroi pantsu haite yagaru kara sagari ni kiku no wa raku da ze!*
  Now that everyone's wearing wider pants, listening down there for wallets is easier!
- *Yā maita ze, jōkyaku minna kenjite mita ga, ii mono nani hitotsu mitsukarya shinē!*
  Man, I groped every single passenger—absolutely nothing worthwhile!
- *Ogande, ogande, yatto yatsu no saifu o mitsuketa ze!*
  I prayed and prayed until I found his wallet!

The most idiosyncratic batch of railroad thieves works out of local trains deep in the provinces. These are young men and women who rummage from car to car doing *kagidasu* (ferreting out), collecting as much plunder as they can. There is no limit to the amount they can collect, because at various strategic points of the journey they open windows and do *nagedasu* (flinging out), which has earned them the name *nagedashizoku* (fling-out gangs). As the train chortles along one of the group, the *dachi* (short for *tomodachi*, "friend"), follows by car, stopping every so often to collect the wallets, bags, and other valuables off the tracks.

4 ▪ Japanese Penises

WHEN VISITING Westerners ask "How do you say penis in Japanese?" or "What's the local word for testicle?" faces turn red, conversations grind to a halt, and bashful friends might even make a dash for the door. Japan's official stance regarding all sexual organs, foreigners often complain, remains "we do not have such words" or "we never say such things." The persistent linguist, however, will keep prodding his acquaintances until they finally give in and admit that there is a slang word, *chinchin*. "But don't ever use it!"

Unconvinced, the seasoned visitors set off for a seedy downtown bar, where they click on their tape recorders and buy round after round after round of drinks. *Chinchin*, they soon discover, is the mild diminutive of harsher words such as *chinpo* and *chinko*, which also appear in the inverted forms *pochin* and *pochi*, favorites in modern red-light neighborhoods. *Dekachin*, a contraction of *dekai* (hulking) and *chinpo* (penis), is used for the well-hung, and *kōkachin*, meaning erect penis, comes from *kōka* (elevated) and *chinpo* (penis). *Yokochin* (side penis) is an organ that generally rests horizontally in its shorts, while *sanpachin* is always worn to the left and thus has a tendency to lean to the side when erect. When a man is wearing boxer shorts or loose swimming trunks and his organ inadvertently pops out, hardened college coeds will point their finger and murmur to each other *yokochin moreru* (the side penis is escaping). *Furuchin* (wagging penis) is an exposed penis.

The madam at the bar sidles over *sotto voce* and whispers that all these penile words came from the tough *chinpoko*, which itself originated from the ante-diluvian *chinhoko* (life-giving sword).

"In the beginning," she explains, "there was Chaos, and the mythical Izanami (the male-who-invites), with the help of his incestuous sister Izanagi, (the female-who-invites), dipped his large *chinhoko* into the ocean. The *chinhoko* was then whisked through the air, the spray flew, and the ancient islands of Japan were created. Amazing, isn't it?"

In the tougher bars of Koganechō, near the port of Yokohama, the foreigner comes face to face with some of the earthiest slang Japan has to offer. Here the local criminal element mixes affably with weather-worn masseuses from the nearby red-light parlors by the train station, local Korean truck drivers, liberated students, corner prostitutes who work in the corru-gated dives under the elevated tracks, and garbage collectors who stop in, between cans, for a quick swig of hot sake. On some nights a Buddhist priest or two might drop by to spice up the atmosphere with a worldly anecdote. Each group in the bar has its own private lingoes and cants, the *ingo* (hidden words) or *ago* (jaw) impenetrable to outsiders. As the mood becomes more convivial, the secret words flow freely and the foreigner can successfully set pen to paper.

The linguist notices that the women in the bar tend

to refer to male organs as sticks. *Konbō* (club), *konebō* (kneading stick), *bō* (rod), *surikogi* (wooden pestle), and *kine* (pounder) are used for large and potent organs, while smaller ones are belittled as *kushi* (skewer), *waribashi* (wooden chopstick), *enpitsu* (pencil), and *hari* (needle). If a man is willing but underendowed, unkind sex masseuses will say he has *ikibari*, a lively needle.

- *Konna ōkii konbō hairanai wa!*
  That big club won't fit in!
- *Konebō o massaji suru toki wa anmari sakimade kawa o hippari agecha dame da yo.*
  When you massage his kneading stick, you shouldn't pull the skin up too high.
- *Ano otoko atashi no hadaka o mita totan, surikogi odoroku hodo ōkiku shichatte!*
  When that man saw me naked his wooden pestle jumped up!
- *Anta kare no chinchikurin na hari mita? Kimochi warui!*
  Did you see his tiny little needle? Gross!
- *Kare atashi ni ikebari sawatte hoshii no yo! Gya!*
  He wanted me to touch his lively needle! Yuck!

When gruff men refer to their penises with stick-like slang words, the images are meatier and more belligerent: *nikubō* (meat rod), *nikubashira* (meat pillar), *tokobashira* (bed pillar), *teppō* (gun), *hoshin* (gun barrel), and *rosen* and *roten*, both rugged fishermen's words for "oar peg." *Roten* was uncovered as a potent slang expression as far back as 1925, when the highbrow Kamigun Kyōiku Kai (Kami County Educational Committee), in their linguistic survey *Kamigunshi*, identified *roten* as being a common Osaka-port word for penis. Another tough masculine trend is to personify the organ. In the post-World War II years the nasty taunt *ketō* (hairy foreigner) became the fashionable word for penis, and the older street crowd still enjoys using it. Organs, after all, are both hairy and, like foreigners, dangle about on the outside (of society, that is). Equating foreigners with penises, everyone agreed, made sense, and as vaginas were increasingly being called *naijin* (inside person) on the streets, what could be punnier than calling penises *gaijin* (outside person), or foreigner.

Other spirited personifications show the organ as being a feisty, independent apprentice, still bound to its master, who has to struggle hard to keep it in check. Words like *deshi* (pupil), *detchi* (apprentice), and *detchibō* (apprentice stick) became the rage. Penises were also referred to as sons: *segare* (my son), *musuko* (son), *emu* (M) the rough school-boy abbreviation of *musuko*, and *san*, the Japanese pronunciation of "son." Sons, the argument goes, are constantly misbehaving. Sometimes one has to even resort to beating them. Cocky words like *bōzu* (sonny) and *yanchabōzu* (naughty little boy), *wagamama na bōzu* (selfish little boy) and *hōtōbōzu* (debauched little boy) became especially popular, as *bōzu* has the added charismaof meaning "priest" and even "a priest's shaven head."

- *Anta musuko shimatte kurenai! Yaru ki shinai kara ne!*
  Put your son away! I'm not in the mood!
- *Mata toire de bōzu o shikoshiko surun ja nai ka!*
  He must be in the toilet again beating his priest!

Another tough group of terms for penis involves

vegetables. *Imo* (potato) is used when organs are short and fat, *tōgarashi* (red pepper) when they are small and pink, and *gobō* (burdock) when they are large and tubular. Umegaki Minoru points out in his book *Ingo* (Hidden Words) that *gobō* has been a favorite since the Middle Ages. *Furuoke de gobō o arau* (washing the burdock in the tub) was considered one of the zestier gauche references to sex. The *matsutake* (mushroom) has a slim shaft and a disproportionately large head; the *rakkyō* (scallion) has an unusually long foreskin that extends well beyond the tip even during an erection, and the *hinedaikon* (shriveled radish) and the *hoshidaikon* (dried radish) are small and very wrinkly. The only garden variety penis in this group is the *kyūri*, a type of cucumber indigenous to Japan that usually grows to a length of approximately four or five inches.

- *Kare no imo oishisō!*
  His pud looks quite tasty!
- *Dō yū shinkei shitenno? Tōgarashi shabure'tte yūn da yo!*
  The nerve! He actually asked me to suck his little dipstick!
- *Hizamazukakete, ore no gobō shaburaseta ze!*
  I made her get on her knees and suck my ramrod!
- *Rakkyō dakara, tatte mo mukenai yo.*
  There's a lotta skin there, so the head stays covered even when it's hard.
- *Hinedaikon mitai dakedo, odoroku hodo ōkiku naru!*
  It might look like a shriveled little radish, but it gets real huge!
- *Ano otoko hoshidaikon muriyari atashi ni ireyō to shita kedō, zenzen muri da yo.*

That man tried to stuff his limp little dick into me, but it just didn't work.

The most prepossessing words bounced about at the bar are the vernacularisms referring to extremely specific traits in an organ. The *kasa* (umbrella) and the *karakasa* (paper parasol), for instance, are penises that are unusually top-heavy. The related *sakibuto* (tip fat) is even more spectacular. Its head is so disproportionately large that it keeps craning out of its foreskin. The *ibo* (pimple), on the other hand, is bottom-heavy, with a thick torso and a very small head. The *insatsumore* (printing error) is an organ that has been completely shaven, while the owner of an *utsubo* is so hairy that his pubic region extends well up beyond the root of his shaft. The *inyake* (penile burn) is dark and debauched. When organs are dangly, growing larger and larger with excitement without, however, manifesting much pith, they are called *chōchin* (paper lanterns), *odawarajōchin* (lanterns from Odawara), *gifujōchin* (large egg-shaped lanterns originally from Gifu), *yowazō* (weak elephants), and *zō no hana* (elephants' trunks).

- *Kinō kita futari no kyaku, ryōhō to mo chōchin datta!*
  I had two clients yesterday who both had long dongs!
- *Atashi honto ni isshōkenmei shabutte shaburimakutta no ni, zenzen yowazō ni kōka nai no!*
  I sucked and sucked till I was blue in the face, but his long dong just wouldn't get hard!

Other eye-catching penises are the *hosomi* (thin body), which is long and spindly, the *namekuji* (slug), which stays soft and small even when excited, and the *burazō* (from *burabura*, "idle"), a floppy organ that is very old. The *rippustikku* (lipstick) is completely covered by foreskin until it is put to use and the glans comes spiraling out, while the *rezāgan* (leather gun) has a remarkably long and crinkly foreskin that often bunches up at the tip. The *rokei* (uncovered root) has a foreskin so short that the glans is constantly gliding out.

The most unfortunate organs are pigeonholed as *hōkei* (covered roots). Their foreskin caps the glans so tightly that penile activity is severely hampered and *kawakiri* (skin cutting), the popular term for the phimosis operation, is called for. The taunting terms for these organs are *menashibō* (eyeless stick), *kawakaburi* (skin covered), *suppon* ("mud turtle," for pull as you may, the head will not come out), and *hōkaburi* and *hōkamuri*, the kind of kerchiefs that Western cow rustlers tied around their faces to keep their incognito.

- *Omae hōkei to kiitan da!*
  We heard you've got problems with your dick!
- *Nani yo sono dekai taidō? Dōse suppon no kuse ni sa!*
  What's with this attitude? His dick doesn't even work right!
- *Nan de atashi no kare anna ni hansamu na no ni, anna ni kawakaburi nan darō.*
  My boyfriend is so handsome, I just wish his dick weren't so useless.
- *Sorya ore hōkaburi dakedō! Dō shiro'ttsūn da yo? Jisatsu shiro'ttsūn no ka yo?*
  So my dick's fucked up! What d'you want me to do? Kill myself?

The bar's male population will often use animalistic words. The largest organs are the *uma* (horse) and the even larger *umaname* (horse lick). These are so sizable that when their owners squat at the public bath, the organs bounce onto the wooden platform in what is admiringly called *itaname* (board licking). Also well-proportioned are the *uwabami* (boa constrictor) and the *aodaishō* (*Elaphe climacophora*), an attractive blue-green snake, and the *orochi*, the mythical monster serpent that never failed to startle ancient heros and heroines. On a smaller scale we find the modest *unagi* (eel), also playfully known as the *miminashiunagi* (earless eel). If a penis is run-of-the-mill the bar crowd will call it a turtle (*kame*) or a goose (*gan* and *kari*). If just the shaft is under discussion, then the more specific *gankubi* and *karikubi*, the words for "goose neck" are used. *Yamagata Hōgen Jiten* (Yamagata Dialect Dictionary), a penetrating linguistic survey published by the Yamagata Dialect Research Association in 1970, holds that in northeastern Japan, in Yamagata, *kari* is used exclusively to specify the lower band of the penile head where the glans is at its widest.

- *Anta no gankubi iren'no? Tetsudate ageru wa?*
  Can't you get your shaft in? You want me to help you?

When an erection is brought up, the goose words are transformed into *gandaka* and *karidaka* (goose high). If the man is fully clothed his friends will laugh, and some will refer to his organ as a *tento mushi* (tent bug), while others will ask tongue in cheek, *Oi, tento o hatteru?* "Yo, you're setting up your tent?"

Some rough bars encourage penile games. After the excited customer has bought the hostess a drink or two, she fumbles for what she girlishly calls his *pinpin-chan* (little Mr. Boing Boing), his erect penis, and does *hakebune* (sailboat). She sits on his lap, squeezes him between her thighs, and rocks back and forth to the cheers and whistles of the crowd. In some of the toughest establishments this bar-stool practice is advertised as *dakko* (dolly), while others go for the more blatant *umanori* (horse riding). Some establishments go even further. They offer *otete supesharu* (handy-pandy special) in which bar women publicly massage customers to orgasm, and *sukinrippu* (skin lip), the post-AIDS-scare attraction in which a penis is double-condomed and then fellated.

These bars are a treasure trove of words for penises. Guffawing men discuss each other's size and prowess, hostesses cackle at their clients' anatomy and purr strings of hushed epithets, the barman reminisces, and the third-generation Korean from Kawasaki city calls his organ *sōbakui*, a favorite term among Tokyo's ethnic Korean gangs. A transvestite recites a chain of fierce words that only gangsters use: *yoshiko, hode, teibo, reji, dekademo, fukubebā, zun, zundoko, sade, bōdō*. Snippets of conversation float through the smoke-filled bar:

- *Boku no sōbakui ga gingin tatchatta!*
  My dork got stiff as a ramrod!
- *Omē no hode shabutchatta?*
  She sucked your cock?
- *Atashi kare no fukubebā ni wa sore hodo kyōmi nain da yo ne.*
  I'm not really that interested in his dong.

- *Onegai dakara! Motto zundoko aratte hoshii nā.*
  You know, I wish you'd wash your dick more often.
- *Atashi shū ni ikkai wa dekademo yan'nai to, ki ga sumanai.*
  If I don't get dick at least once a week I go nuts.
- *Kanojo ore no bōdō massaji suru no ga umain da yo. Ore nifun de itchimau yo.*
  She's real good at massaging my stick. Two minutes and I shoot my wad.

As the linguists listen, they are convinced that some of the heavy slang words must have ancient roots. After all, they muse, in English we've been using "cock" since the fifteenth century, "staff" since the sixteenth, "sausage" and "stick" since the seventeeth, "dick," "gherkin," "banana," and "shlong" since the nineteeth, and the American favorites "dork" and "dong" since the 1920s.

Obashira (male pole), *odogu* (male tool), *ohashi* (male edge) and its derivative *ohasse*, definitely smack of the Middle Ages, as do the bellicose *yari* (spear), *suyari* (naked spear), *tsuchi* (sledgehammer), *sakasaboko* (upside-down sword), and *tsuka* ("handle," as in knife handle, or "hilt," as in hilt of a sword). *Nukimi* (drawn sword) and *danbira* (broad sword) must also have been handed down from medieval times, as no one in the bar would have had much occasion to see a sword of any kind.

An even older group of tough words center around the Buddhist expression *mara*, a word of Sanskrit pedigree which is reputed to have arrived in Japan with the first Buddhist doctrines in the mid-sixth century A.D. In its original guise, *mara* referred to the dangerous demon of worldly cravings that disrupted the priests' serene meditations, thus spoiling their chance of attaining the enlightenment of nirvana and Buddhahood. Most ecclesiastics managed to steer clear of forbidden delicacies, such as the occasional drink or the occasional mouthful of meat, but when it came to the hardest temptation, the stirring of the flesh, many tottered. A single lewd thought, however fleeting, was enough to push the cleric off the narrow path to illumination. As ever-longer lines of priests tried to secure Buddhahood by enrolling for *rasetsu* (cutting off the demon), *mara* entered into monastic slang as one of the many priestly words for penis.

Throughout the nineteenth century *mara* was snatched up nationwide by the bar-and-tavern crowd as modern priests, eager to socialize, spilled out of their monasteries and into the streets. *Konseimara* (golden life penis) became the word for a perfectly proportioned organ, and *dekamara* (hulking penis) was used to describe penises that are particularly large. An excited organ that is neither too hard nor too soft was classed as *fumara*, and a large but flabby organ, *funyamara* (floppy penis). *Furimara* (dangling penis), is a penis that unintentionally plops out of its shorts in public. Bentenmaru Takashi, in his 1932 book *Ishinomakiben*, maintained that in some regions of Miyagi *furimara* (dangling penis) had, surprisingly enough, acquired gender equality. Depending on the context, *Arya furimara dambe* can mean both he or she "is not wearing anything under there." In modern brothel slang, *sumara* (naked penis) refers to an uncondomed penis, while *sakamara* (alcohol penis), *happamara* (marijuana penis), and *yakumara* (drug penis) are used for organs that are too crapulous to be of use.

Mara has even been absorbed into the slang speech of the most distant mountain dialects. In the northeastern Tohoku region, for instance, a rough village word for penis is *marafuguri* (penis testicle), while *marafuri* (penile wag) is used for naked men.

On the other side of Japan, on some of the islands of Okinawa, *marafuri* means "penis dangle," i.e. "penis and testicles." *Marafuri* is used when the speaker is discussing the whole sexual organ, as opposed to just the shaft and the glans.

As tourists from the Japanese mainland often realize too late, *mara* on many of the outlying islands exclusively refers to testicles.

When *mara* is scrawled onto bathroom walls today, it is brushed on with the labyrinthine twenty-one-stroke character *ma* (demon) followed by the nineteen-stroke *ra* (contain). But some graffiti artists pronounce this choice of characters bogus, and compose *mara* with the fifteen-stroke *ma* (rub) and the nineteen-stroke *ra* (contain). A penis, they protest, needs to be rubbed to be contained. Others who cannot manage the complex brush patterns go for the simplest solution of all: five strokes for *ma* (tip) and thirteen strokes for *ra* (naked).

The madam sidles over once more to the group of linguists and confides that even hoarier words will pop up at the bar.

"Take 'dozen' for example," she says. "Today a garbage collector will use it as a smutty allusion to a penis. Back in the glamorous days of the samurai, however, it was a perfectly legitimate word for a man's head."

"Then there is *mameyakamono*," she continues. "Today it's a crass organ that bounces up at the slightest provocation, while medieval novelists used it to mean 'robust chap'."

She offers some examples:

- *Atashi kare no dozen ga haitte kuru mae ni, rōshon nuranai to dame na no!*
  Before he puts his man's head in I always rub some lotion on it.
- *Kare no dozen no katachi kirāai! Kimochi warui!*
  I hate the shape of his man's head! It's gross!
- *Atashi kare no mameyakamono ga pantsu no naka de dekaku naru no wakatchatta.*
  I could tell his robust individual was getting hard in his pants.

At the other end of the bar there is a group of lively students, whose hair is tightly permed and dreadlocked. Their new bellbottomed jeans are very wide, with many little bright patches carefully handsewn onto where the fabric might one day tear. Some are wearing Nigerian skull caps, others tall and colorful Jamaican wool hats. These are the *burazazoku* (brother gang), also known as *burakkuzoku* (black gang), and *bobii-kun* (little Mr. Bobby-men, after the musician Bobby Brown). These gangs slavishly disguise themselves as African Americans, thread their language with as much English as possible, and hang out in wrecked neighborhood dives, where they keep to themselves and pretend they are in an *ōruburakku* (all black) bar somewhere deep in New York. Their speech is speckled with tilted expletives such as *sanadabichi* (son of the bitch), *shittoman* (shit man), and *mazāfakingu* (mother fucking). When asked for a list of the coolest scene words for "penis," they recite the strings of quasi-American words popular in Tokyo's progressive inner-city high schools and colleges. The first word to jump up is *burakkujakku* (black jack), along with *burakkubatto* (black bat). These are strong and elephantine organs. Other powerful Tokyo-American words are *sukuryū* (screw), *pisuton* (piston), *magunamu* (magnum), and *bōringu* ("boring," the Japanese for boring machine or drill). The erudite *farosu* (phallus) and the earthy *kokku* (cock) are also used. When a penis is exceptionally gifted it is called *chāji* (battery charge), and if it is not it is called a *moderugan* (model gun)—it might look like a lethal weapon but it is quite harmless. The smallest penises are called *pākā* (Parker), after the pen.

The single most diehard student word for penis has been *emu*, the initial "M." During the late nineteenth century, in the Meiji period, when Japan for the first time opened up to the West, students discovered the Latin alphabet and quickly put all its letters to trendy slang use. *Esu*, (S) came to mean "pretty," from the German word *schoen*; *bii*, stood for "back" as in ass, and a pert combination like *bii esu* (BS) stood for *back schoen* (nice ass). The single favorite fin-de-siècle letter, however, was "M," short for the intriguing and contorted *menburumu biriirisu* (membrum virilis). For decades the protracted Latin word was the rage. Everyone knew it but no one could pronounce it, until one day the word lost its novelty and the students began using "M" for the more circumspect "member" (as in male member). Later "M" came to represent the earthier *mara* (penis), and in today's colleges the euphemistic *mono* (thing) and *musuko* (son).

- *Ano ko kangaeteru koto to ittara burakkujakku no koto bakari!*
  All that girl is interested in is black jack!
- *Aitsu no sukuryū wa dore gurai ōkii?*
  How big is his screw?
- *Aitsu kane haratta to shite mō, atashi moderugan nanka sawaru monka!*
  I wouldn't touch his model gun if you paid me!
- *Ore no emu biichi ni ittara dekaku natchimatta! Hazukashikatta, mina jirojiro mita!*
  At the beach my "M" got hard! I was so embarrassed, everyone was staring!

5 ▪ Urban Vaginas

WESTERNERS LIVING in Japan often complain that Japanese friends, business associates, and acquaintances go out of their way to shield them from *warui kotoba* (bad words). The sexier the words, the stronger the shield. When the foreigner finally asks, "Excuse me, how do you say 'vagina' in Japanese?" even the trendiest Tokyoites will goggle, turn red, and splutter, "we never say such things in Japanese." But after five or six rounds of drinks the barriers of linguistic propriety begin to crumble. "*Asoko* (over there) is the word you're looking for," the foreign guest is told. "*Kanojo no asoko*, her 'over there', is what we say. But don't ever use it!"

After a few more drinks, the medical term *chitsu* is bounced about, followed by the dictionary entry *joseiki* (female instrument), after which the subject is changed.

At this point, foreigners who wish to pursue the matter further must stalk words through back streets and dark alleys. They must trudge through slums, through fish markets, past rows and rows of noisy street-vendor stalls; they must follow dump trucks on their rounds, hang out at shady local bars, buy hoodlums drinks, and then footslog from high school yard to youth center, from video arcade to *yakitori* grill to pachinko parlor.

As the tourists penetrate deeper into the street scene, they realize that each clique has its own specialized words, particularly when it comes to sexual organs. Trendy highschoolers favor clever puns, naughty college students prefer foreign words, the motorcycle gang likes the tough traditional words of the local mob, and the local mob has its own proud roster of historic expressions that often date back centuries to Edo period speech. Among downtown musicians, for instance, one of the more popular words for vagina is *kiigā*, an inversion of *gakki* (musical instrument).

- *Nā, anta no kiigā hikitē!*
  Ooh, would I like to pluck your instrument!
- *Aitsu no kiigā wa itsumo jitojito da ze!*
  Her instrument is always wet and ready!

The fishmongers of Tokyo's Tsukiji market favor *suji*, as in "muscle" or "sinew." The prostitutes of the soapland bathhouses call their organs *kanebako* (money box). Even Buddhist priests have a private and sacrilegious slang all their own. A deep vagina, for instance, is called *saiijintai* (the ultimate depth), while a *sōshiki manjū*, a funeral bun (uncommonly wide when compared to regular buns) is used for extremely large vaginas. A *manibachi* (clerical pot) is a Buddhist nun's organ. As with all tight-knit slang groups, one must be an insider in order to follow the Buddhist's rap.

- *Sazanami ni wa chigainai ga, genkan de isha to bōzu ga matteta no sa.*
  Even though the waves were rippled, both doctor and priest were waiting at her gate.
  (Even though her face was all wrinkled, both my finger and my penis were ready to enter her vagina.)

The four most popular rude words for vagina in Japan are *omanko* in central and northern Japan, *omeko* in central and southern Japan, *bebe* in the north, and *bobo* in the south. As one begins mingling with different sets of people, these staple words start falling by the wayside. In school yards, *omanko* is transformed by tough girls into *miiman*, with "me" (as in myself) joined to the *man* of *omanko*.

- *Iikagen ni shite yo! Miiman sawaranaide!*
  Cut the crap! Don't touch my twat!
- *Biichi ni iku to miiman ni suna ga ippai hairu kara, iya nan da yo na.*
  What I hate about going to the beach is that I get sand up my twat.

When even rougher teenage girls wish to casually chat about vaginas they will use *omanman*, *omunmun*, and *omonmon*, while their more refined peers prefer the dubious expressions *wareme* (crack) and *wareme-chan*, (little Miss Crack). Both terms are comfortably used by teachers in sex education classes throughout Japan.

With-it school speech is full of English expressions and secret codes. "HT," short for "half think," means you love someone but he or she totally ignores you. An "FM" is a "fuck mate," an "HB" a "homo boy," and an "F" a "feminine"—what American MTV might call a dazzler or a babe. Most of the hottest 1990s' words for the female organ are of English extraction: *rōzu* (rose), *kanū* (canoe), *biibā* (beaver), *kurebasu* (crevice), and even *kurētā* (crater) are rampant in fashionable school yards.

- *Busu da'tte ii ja nē ka! Rōzu wa rōzu nan da mon!*
  So what if she's a dog! A rose is a rose!
- *Kare atashi no kanū zutto shita de nametsuzukete, mō saikō dattan dakara!*
  He was licking my canoe like crazy! Ooh, it felt great!
- *Aitsu biibā yoku aratte kara beddo ni haitte kita.*
  First she washed her beaver and then she got into bed.
- *Chotto sono yubi kurebasu kara hazushite, honmono irete kun'nai!*
  Will you get your finger out of my crevice and put the real thing in!

Raunchy schoolboy magazines like *Sukora* (Scholar) and *Dokkiri Shashin* (Surprise Pictures), also read by college freshmen and other young men, have done much to strengthen the young Japanese male's grip on would-be international sex words. Words like *bokkusu* (box), a direct translation of the street favorite *hako*, are packaged in those bouncy magazines with the even more arcane *deruta* (delta) and *derutachitai* (delta zone). Topping the loanword list in popularity is *chikin* (chicken).

- *Boku kanojo no deruta mitchimata ze! Sugē!*
  I saw her delta! Awesome!
- *Ore kanojo no pantsu no shita no migoto na chikin sōzō shitchau yo nā.*
  I can just imagine her luscious chicken under those panties of hers.

Handy English terms like *cherii furawā* (cherry flower) and *pinku* (pink) can be used for both virgins and virginal vaginas, while *kizumono* (broken thing) and *sekonhan* (secondhand) are used for more experienced women and non-virginal organs. *Kirimanjaro suru* (doing Mount Kilimanjaro) is an upbeat and popular pun for breaking a virgin's hymen. *Kiri* means "cut," *man* is "vagina," and *jaro* is left on the end to clinch the naughty word game. Tougher boys, however, use tougher words such as *shiunten* (test drive) and *fūgiri* (premiere).

- *Ore zettai kono gakkō ni cherii furawā hitori mo inai to omou yo!*
  I don't think there's a single virgin left in this school!
- *Aitsu wa shojo to bakkari omotteta kedo, jitsu wa kizumono datta ze.*
  I was convinced she was a virgin, but it turned out she had a broken thing.
- *Omae, ano onna kirimanjaro shita daro?*
  You're the one who popped that woman's cherry, right?
- *Yūbe no shiunten yoku nakatta kara, suteta.*
  The test drive last night wasn't that good, so I dumped her.

Organs of the Tokyo Back Alleys

As one leaves the schoolyard and heads for the restaurant and bar area of the downtown back alleys and slums, terms for the female sexual organ become more traditional. One of the most notorious groups of words is of pot-and-pan background, with favorites like *ochawan* (tea bowl), *ochaire* (teapot), *tsubo* (canister), *usu* (mortar), *hachi* (bowl), *utsuwa* (utensil), and *hako* (box).

- *Omē kanojo no ochawan mita?*
  Did you get to see her tea bowl?
- *Kanojo mata hirote, ore ni tsubo miseta.*
  She spread her thighs and showed me her canister.
- *Ano gaijin no suke ii hako shiteru ze.*
  That foreign chick has one great box.

Other potent pantry expressions are *nukabukuro* (rice-bran bag), *nabe* (cookpot), and *kobako* (small box). These words for vagina have flourished since the Edo period, and have been sharpened by centuries of persistent use. A feisty old-time urban expression for the organs of extremely provincial girls, for instance, was *donabe* (mud pot), while *akanabe* (red cookpot), is still used by brusque gangsters to refer to menstruating organs.

- *Akanabe da ga, yatchimaō ze!*
  Even though your cooking pot is red, let's go ahead with it!

Tsubo (canister) will often pop up in rough speech

along with *chatsubo* (tea canister), which in nineteenth century slang was used exclusively for organs perfumed with aromatic spices, a connotation that has been lost in modern times.

- *Kane o jūbun ni harattara, ano onna chatsubo teikyō shite kureru ze.*
  If you give that woman enough money, she'll let you have a go at her tea canister.

Words of the same family that are popular with tougher, older mobsters are *sumitsubo* (ink pot), *fuigo* (bellows), *hikeshitsubo* (charcoal extinguisher), and *nikutsubo* (meat jar).

The group of pot-related words comes in especially handy when the speaker needs to add a descriptive edge to his statement. When women shave their pubic region, the ceramic word used is *kawarake*, an unglazed earthen cup. *Ochoko*, a tiny sake cup, represents an unduly tight organ, while *osara*, a narrow dish, suggests that the organ is extremely shallow. *Meiki* (exquisite article) is used for organs that are top-notch.

- *Ore osara'tte suki nan da yo na. Tenjō made tsukeru kara na.*
  I really like a small dish, 'cause you bump against the ceiling.
- *Kanojo no ochoko dakara, ireru no o itakute yō!*
  Her thing's so tight, it really hurts when I put it in!
- *Sawatte mita toki, kanojo no meiki mō bichobicho datta yo.*
  When I felt her exquisite article, it was already hot and juicy.

When an organ is large and wet, *tarai* (basin), *ohachi* (rice tub), *furo* (bathtub), and the harsher *nikuburo* (meat tub) are used. The largest organs on the street are labeled *ōzara* (platter), and the largest of all *todana* (cupboard).

- *Aitsu no nikuburo no tekuniku wa saikō dakara, omae kondo tameshite minai yo?*
  She sure knows how to use that meat tub of hers. Why don't you try her out sometime?
- *Bājin? Omae nani'tten da yo! Aitsu wa todana da ze!*
  A virgin? Gimme a break! Her thing's like a cupboard!

Just as the slangiest English expressions for vagina have histories that stretch back to early medieval times ("cunt," 1300s, "twat," 1500s), many of modern Japan's earthier equivalents are just as ancient. The largest body of taboo words to have survived the centuries unscathed is the shellfish group. Words like *kai* (shell), *yohamaguri* (night clam), *yakihamaguri* (baked clam), *kani* (crab), and the coarser *kegani* (hairy crab), can be heard sweeping through heated discussions in late-night sushi dives, early-morning fish markets, and all the rougher downtown bars and groggeries. The shellfish words, many find, are especially useful when a specific type of vagina is brought up. *Karasugai* (fresh-water mussel shell), for instance, is used when a woman has very dense pubic hair; *karasugai* literally means "raven shell." The clam (*hamaguri*) is a large organ with a strong sphincter, while the corbicula shell (*shijimi*) and the surf clam (*shiofuki*) are both small and tight. (*Shiofuki*, "salt spray," is also the jet of water that a whale spouts, which has given it its second slang meaning of "hefty spurts of sperm.")

- *Omae kanojo ni sake ogottara, sukunakutomo kai sawarashite moraeru ze.*
  If you're buying her a drink she should at least let you feel her shell.
- *Atashi sanfujinka no shinsatsu daikirai! Hamaguri ni nanka tsukkomareru kara nē.*
  I hate going to the gynecologist! He always puts things up my clam.
- *Kanojo no kegani nuretete junbi okkē datta!*
  Her hairy crab was wet and ready!

Kai (shell) has given birth to a whole line of raffish expressions. In the Middle Ages, saucy novellas kept readers on edge with words like *shakogai* (clam shell), *ikigai* (living shell), and, when an organ was stunningly large, *horagai* (trumpet shell). In Yoshiwara, Tokyo's old pleasure quarter, *shinkai* (new shell) was used for virgins, while *takaragai*, (jewel shell), referred to the worldly organs of the top courtesans. The medieval *awasegai* (meeting shells), has turned in modern speech into *kaiawase* (shell meeting), and is one of Japan's coarser expressions for lesbian sex. Another idiom that has survived the centuries is *kaisenzuri* (shell thousand-rubs). It remains today a potent motorcycle-gang word for female masturbation.

- *Atashi, kaiawase? Nanitten da yo!*
  Me, bump pussy? Please!
- *Ano ko-tachi zenbu suru no: rap dansu, kaisenzuri, zenbu.*

Those bar girls do everything: lap dancing, solo-fingering, everything.

Tokyoites touring southern Japan are often stunned to hear farmers in the rural outbacks using *kai* exclusively to discuss their cows' vaginas. In his penetrating 1937 publication, *Zoku Ikishima Hōgenshū*, linguist Yamagata indicates that *kai* has been used for cows as far south as Nagasaki. Almost three decades later, in 1969, after an extensive period of probing field work, the Kamo Kyōdoshi Linguistic Research Committee, in their publication *Kamoda ni Kotoba*, finally set the Okayama province as the bovine *kai's* northern boundary.

Akagai (ark shell) is one of the most versatile slang words for vagina. Many speakers use it as a straightforward reference to the organ, with the idea that the shell (*kai*) is red (*aka*) in color. A more picaresque crowd uses the red shell for older organs. *Saragai* (new shell) would be that of a chaste teenager, while *akagai*, flushed and red, has achieved a rich hue through years of experience. Still others use *akagai* to refer to an organ in orgasm. In the fiercest urban slang speech the red shell symbolizes a menstruating organ.

- *Kyō atashi no akagai dakara, ushiro kara shite.*
  My shell is red today, let's do it from behind.
- *Hayaku, tampon chōdai! Akagai ni natta kara.*
  Quick, gimme a tampon! My shell's turning red.

Even Buddhist priests are not above inventing their own shell idioms, and after a few drinks (a practice strongly discouraged by doctrine), baser street words are often touched up with a few lofty religious terms. *Nōkai* (gifted shell), for instance, is an experienced vagina, while the euphonious *makakai* is made up of the Sanskrit *maha*, "great" (as in maharajah, great king), and *kai* (shell). Pleasant organs are referred to as *kairen* (lotus shell), while unpleasant ones are called *kunkai* (odoriferous shell). Polite priests, however, will use the more elegant *keishu* (firefly scented).

- *Yō mani demo, nōkai wa hitome de wakaru mon da yo.*
  Even when leaves cover the demon nun, I can tell at a glance if a shell's gifted.
  (Even if she's wearing panties, I can tell with a glance if she's got good pussy.)
- *Ano hito no makagai ni ogamitai mono desu yo.*
  I'd kneel in prayer before her divine shell any day.
- *Kanojo wa kunkai dakara, watashi wa enryo shit'okimasu yo.*
  I think I'll keep my distance—her shell is odoriferous.

Kaidan (shell discourse) in clerical circles refers to risqué banter. *Takai* (shell banging) is the priestly word for intercourse, *kaimō* (shell hair) is a woman's pubic region, and *tonkai* (hasty shell) is hurried sex. In *kaisaku* (shell quest), the priest rubs and even penetrates a female organ with his fingers. When a priest peeks through a window with the help of binoculars, the practice is known as *kaimaku* (curtained shells).

- *Anta no toshi de kaimaku shinagara shoshagyō suru to wa!*
  At your age observing curtained shells while copying out sutras!

(At your age to be peeking and playing with yourself, really!)

Dongai (shell coveter) is a priest who is excessively interested in female organs.

* * *

After scouring through school grounds, dump-truck yards, monasteries, and downtown dives, the linguists venture into rougher neighborhoods ready to seek out and interview the fiercest urban gangsters, the Yakuza. Since the government's anti-mob activities of 1993 and 1994 these gangsters have become less visible, but once contact has been made, the Westerners are surprised at the scintillating private vocabularies they encounter among different gangs.

The Yakuza hierarchy runs the gamut from the most junior members, the *chinpira* (pricks) and the tough *teppodama* (bullets), usually in their twenties, all the way up to the grand *oyabun* (paternal part), the gang's godfather. Each gang level has its favorite words. When it comes to vaginas, the Yakuza gangs turn out to be a repository of old and elegant idioms, with generation after generation of gangsters learning the rigid classical jargon of their elders. Beautiful expressions like *shumon* (orange gate), *saya* (sheath), *fuji-san* (Mount Fuji), and even *maku no uchi* ("behind the curtains," curtains in this case referring to the woman's panties), dot the speech of the most ruthless criminals.

- *Tsugi ni ore sā, ano ko no shumon ni yubi suberasetan da.*

Then the next thing I did was to stick my fingers up her orange gate.

- *Ore ga itta ato, kanojo jibun de saya fuite yagatta.*
  After I came she wiped her own sheath.
- *Ano ko wa sonna kantan ni fuji-san akewatasu yō na onna ja nai yo.*
  She's not the type of woman to give her Mount Fuji away so easily.

Yakuza slang is fanatically nationalistic and steers clear of foreign words, especially when it comes to vaginas. Even the youngest Yakuza recruits, fresh out of high school, avoid trendy American imports such as *pushii* (pussy) and *suritto* (slit). When given the choice in referring to vaginas, Japanese slang speakers generally prefer using terms for salty sea creatures. Among the Yakuza novices, however, some of the most popular words for the female organ involve fruits: *momo* (peach), sometimes referred to by rougher boys as *kemomo* (hair peach), *suika* (watermelon), *uri* (melon), the Japanese *akebi* fruit, and *amaguri* (roasted chestnut). *Ichijiku* (fig) is the only fruit that the young Yakuza also tolerate in its English form, *fuiku*.

- *Nā! Ano onna no toshi de kemomo nureru to omou ka?*
  Tell me, d'you think her snatch still gets wet at her age?
- *Kono bokashi tondemo nē yo na! Ore honmono no suika ga mitai yo!*
  Man, this censoring is too much! I wanna see some real watermelon!
- *Shinjirareru ka? Kanojo kurutta yō ni ichijiku ijikuri-mawashiteta!*

Would you believe it? She was frigging away at her fig like crazy!

- *Atashi fuiku ni atarashii kokeshi irete mitan dakedo— sugoi yokatta wa!*
  I stuck that new vibrator up my fig—it was ace!

As gangsters get older, the words they use for the female organ get heftier. In middle-aged criminal circles fruity idioms give way to boggy, marshy images such as *numa* (swamp), *oka* (hill), *otoshiana* ("pitfall," for very large organs), *tani* (valley), and *ichi no tani* (first valley).

- *Ore-tachi sutorippā no numa nogashita ya na. Pantii nuganēn da mon!*
  We didn't get to see the stripper's swamp. She kept her panties on!

- *Atarashii sutorippā no otoshiana mita? Sugē!*
  Did you see the new stripper's pitfall? Hot!

The single most fashionable swamp word in the underworld is the ancient *yachi* (bog). In some gang jargons *yachi* appears in its inverted form *chiya*, which has also developed into a shorter form, *cha*. Over the centuries *yachi* has given rise to a remarkable list of organ-related expressions: *yachigakushi* (bog hiding), for instance, is one of the rougher words for panties, and *yachineta* (bog news) is pornography. *Yachihakui* (bog in white) is the accomplished organ of a mature woman, while *yachikoro* (rolling the bog), *yachiseme* (invading the bog), *yachikameru* (crawling into the bog), and *yachikeri* (plowing the bog), are rowdy words for sex. *Yachigari* (twat kid) is a harsh and very unkind name for a pre-teen girl.

- *Aitsu no yachigari mo mō shōgakusei kā? Jikan ga tatsu no wa ha'ē mon da.*
  Is his little twat already in elementary school? Man, time flies.
- *Ano yachigari ga ore no kao ni notte kuretara, shinde mo ii yo!*
  If that twat kid rode my face, dying would be perfectly fine!
  (Man! That little twat can ride my face any day!)

An interesting phenomenon of the nineties has been the snowballing of the secondhand soiled-panty trade. Boutiques with names like Atene, Q-tii, and Tiffany have opened throughout Japan, catering to the *shitagimania* (underwear maniacs). These are cliques of middle-aged and elderly men who enjoy buying up heaps of used panties, bras, and skirts. The more soiled the item, i.e., the longer it has been worn, the higher the price. If a panty is billed as having been the property of a woman over twenty, trade jargon calls it *yachibira* (twat poster), or *yachihi*. If the former owner was well under twenty, the clothes (anything from badly peed-into underwear to full-fledged, sweat-stained school uniforms) are referred to as *yachigaribira* (twat-kid posters).

The deeper one penetrates the street scene, the tougher the *yachi* words become. *Yachi o hegu* (flaying the bog) and *yachi o sogu* (mutilating the bog) are two of the most raucous Japanese terms for rape. *Yachibai* (bog trade) and *yachiuri* (bog sale) refer to prostitution, while *yachikai* (bog purchase) means buying a prostitute. In the underworld when a man is a sex maniac he is *yachimoro* (bog fragile), or even *yachigure* (bog lost).

- *Yachikai ni ikō?*
  Shall we pick up a hooker?
- *Tai no onna ga haitte kite irai, yachibai wa noborichōshi da yo!*
  Since the Thai girls have come in, cunt sales have really gone up!
- *Aitsu minato de yachiuri yatteru rashii ze.*
  I think she sells cunt down in the port.
- *Imadoki eizu no mondai mo aru'tte no ni sōpu ni yachimoro iku nante omae mo taishita tama da na.*
  What with the AIDS problem and all, you've sure got guts to keep on going down to the soapland bathhouses like some lech.
- *Naomi ni atte irai, aitsu wa yachigure 'chimatta ze. Sō darō?*
  Since he met Naomi he's become a total sex maniac. Don't you think so?

The idioms for vagina used by the oldest members of the Yakuza mob, the top of the underworld hierarchy, are calmer, more stately, and exude a strong traditional flavor. The vagina becomes the speaker's *kokyō* (native place), or *furusato* (birthplace), *sato* for short.

- *Mō ano babā no kokyō wa akiaki da ze!*
  I'm bored sick of that old bitch's native place!
- *Chotto sukāto makutte miro yo! Furusato sawatte yaru kara sa.*
  Lift your skirt a bit! I wanna feel your birthplace.

Other powerful and elderly vocabulary is *obake* (ghost), *okame*, a smiling fat-faced woman's mask used in Kabuki theater, and the strange but popular expression *waraji* (straw sandals).

- *Na! Oji-chan wa omē no waraji ni shita tsukkomashite kure yo!*
  C'mon, let uncle lick your straw sandals!

6 ▪ Provincial Vaginas

TRAVELING THE whole length of Japan, from northern Hokkaido to southern Okinawa, enquiring tourists are stunned by the variety and vibrancy of the slang words they encounter for the female organ. Although urban acquaintances back in Tokyo might have warned them that the Japanese, especially in the provinces, never refer directly to sexual organs, as the travelers make their way from village to village questioning farmers, field hands, truck drivers, and local housewives, the list of unspeakable words grows and grows.

The two most prominent Japanese words for vagina are *omanko* and *omeko*. *Omanko*, along with its shorter form *manko*, has its linguistic seat in the Tokyo area and is popular throughout all the northern provinces as far as the port city of Hakodate on Hokkaido. *Omeko*'s domain is the south, from the cities of Nagoya, Osaka, and Kyoto, down to the island of Kyushu.

As one drives from Tokyo to the northern tip of Honshu, *omanko* appears with different lilts. On the street corners of Fujiyoshida, west of Tokyo, one hears the curt *oma*; in nearby Kōfu city it is the drawn-out *omanchō*, while in the more isolated regions of northern Gunma, *omanko* is used alongside *ochanko*, which in its turn has developed in neighboring areas into *chanko, ochako, chako* (*cho*, for short). In the western province of Ishikawa it even appears as *chancha* and *chacha*.

In the south, *omeko* is dominant. Its territory stretches from the Kansai region all the way down to the isolated Pacific fishing villages of Miyazaki on the island of Kyushu. Like *omanko*, its northern rival, *omeko* comes in many regional forms. On the streets of Hiroshima, for instance, it has evolved into *omechō, omenchō* (sometimes also pronounced *omencho*), and in some districts *omencha, omecha,* and *mencha*. In Kobe, the sharper *ome* is often preferred in rough street speech, while fifty miles down the road, in the seaside province of Tottori, *omeko* is used with deference, while its local variations *omecha, omencho,* and *mencho* spring up in raunchier conversations.

Further down, on the coastal roads of Shimane, the northern *omanko* and the southern *omeko* meet. The result is *omenko*, which, as one drives between the seaside towns of Hamada and Masuda, is transformed into *menko, meme,* and even *memeko*. In Kōchi, on the island of Shikoku, both *meko* and *manko* are used interchangeably without the honorific prefix "*o*," while on the nearby island of Kyushu, *omeko* has evolved into *meicho, meme, meme-jo* (*meme*-woman), *meme-ko* (*meme*-girl), *meme-san* (Ms. Meme), and even *meme-sama* (Lady Meme).

- *Aitsu to wa nagaku tsukiatō kedo, mada ikkai mo omeko mita koto nai tai.*
  Even though we've been dating for a long time, I've never seen her twat.

- *Honna kotsu! Aitsu ikkai mo meicho yarashite kuren ken nē!*
  Man! She never lets me put it in her twat!
- *Meme-jo kakusan' to minna ni mirareru bai?*
  Come on, cover your twat! D'you want everyone to see it?

The traveling linguist quickly realizes that Japanese dialectology is full of pitfalls. No sooner has a taboo word been netted in one village than it tends to reappear a few miles down the road with a completely different meaning. *Ikimi* (breathing body) in the northern prefecture of Aomori means "vagina"; in Akita, sixty miles away, local hoodlums use it exclusively to discuss anuses. In Miyagi, *bekya* is an ordinary vagina, while a few miles north, in Iwate, *bekeā* or *bekyā* is a shaved organ. In southern Japan, *meko* and *menko* are unmentionably crass words for vagina; in the mountains of northern Japan *meko* or *menko* is a pretty and well-behaved pre-teen girl. *Okama*, a word for iron pot that has been nationally appropriated to mean "homosexual," is used in Tochigi and Gunma for "vagina," and in other areas further south for "anus." Then in some areas of Gifu, in central Japan, *okama* turns into a brawny and politically incorrect provincial word for "physically challenged," while in other areas of Gifu *okama! okama!* means "mommy! mommy!"

The case of *betcho* is even more bizarre. Throughout much of northeastern Japan, in such provinces as Yamagata, Miyagi, and Fukushima, *betcho*, *betchō*, *becho*, and *bechō* serve as uncouth references to the female organ. In some areas of Fukushima, however, *betcho* refers to sex, while eight provinces away, in

Shimane, villagers use *bechō* to discuss virginal organs and *benchō* for those more mature. The group of *betcho* words then completely disappears from the map until, hundreds of miles away, on Kyushu island, *betcho* resurfaces as an uncouth reference to a bowel movement.

- *Aitsu kōen de betcho shiotcha nai t'ya.*
  He must be in the park taking a shit again.
- *Mō! Betcho shita ato wa chanto nagasan to ikan bai!*
  Man! If you're gonna take a shit, at least flush afterwards!

Another central Japanese word for the female organ that drastically changes meaning as it moves south is *heko*. Its furthest northern domain is Akita, where it appears both as *heko* and *hekko*. Going south, however, *heko* reappears in Chiba, near Tokyo, in Kagawa on Shikoku island, and in Kyushu as a male g-string, while in Hiroshima *hekō* is an underskirt.

Japanese linguists are still baffled as to why *heko* became a favored provincial word for vagina, and over the years different linguistic camps have offered wildly differing etymological possibilities. In a forgotten 1847 study, published by the Edo period linguist Ono, *heko* is featured as a southern Kyushu word for "the pink meaty underbelly of a crab." Almost a century later, in 1937, Yamaguchi in his book *Zoku Ikishima Hōgenshū*, confirms that throughout the fisheries of Nagasaki, *heko* refers to the soft and edible part of a shell.

Among the most versatile regional slang words are *heppe* and *tanbe*. In the northern port of Hakodate both words are frequently used by local dockworkers and sailors in discussing vaginas. Further south, *heppe* becomes a penis, then a testicle, then sexual intercourse, and then a vagina again. *Tanbe*, also pronounced *danbe* and *tanpe*, is even more flexible. In Yamagata slang *danbe* is a large and in some cases erect penis; in the coastal areas of Shimane some fishermen use it for anus, others for vagina, others again for penis, while street cliques in the seaside town of Masuda use it to taunt obese individuals. *Danbe* is at its most ductile in Niigata in central Japan. Locals there are very surprised to hear that their northern neighbors use it for vaginas. *Danbe*, they argue, is a hanging, swingy thing: a testicle, a penis, the pendulum of a grandfather clock, and in some farming villages even the dangly dewlap of a rooster— but never a vagina. Other Niigatans again, insist that *danbe* does not dangle but is a round, soft, and pulpy thing: a wad of cow dung, a jellyfish, a persimmon, or a testicle. Only a flabby and very small ball-like penis could possibly qualify as *danbe*. Then in Sado, on Niigata's seafront, in the bars and the pubs of the port, *danbe* takes on yet another form. *Danbe ni naru* (becoming *danbe*) means drinking oneself under the table.

After *omanko* and *omeko*, the two most prominent words nationwide for the female organ are *bebe* and *bobo*. In his controversial book *Nihongo wa Doko Kara Kita ka?* (Where Does Japanese Come From?), the popular Japanese linguist Kawasaki Shinchi argues that both these words are of ancient Egyptian provenance. Japan, his theory goes, was colonized by Egyptian adventurers. As a result, unbeknownst to modern street cliques, many of their favorite words for vagina are of Egyptian origin. In more modern times *bobo* and *bebe*, propelled by their pleasant alliterative sound, have spread into provincial street speech throughout Japan.

Bobo is of southern origin, a Kyushu island word, but it appears side by side with *bebe* in dialects all the way from Shikoku island to the opium plains of Tsugaru in the extreme northern part of Honshu. In many areas *bobo* is considered far crasser than *bebe*. While with-it Tokyoites might enjoy bandying *bobo* about in their club-scene speech, even the toughest of street gangs in Fukuoka and Nagasaki will use it with the greatest circumspection.

- *Aitsu ni sakaya de ippai ogottara, bobo misete kureru'tte shittotta ya!*
  D'you know, if you buy her a lotta drinks at the bar, she'll show you her twat!
- *Kono kuriimu o bobo ni nuttara ninshin sen kai na?*
  If I rub this cream into my cunt I won't get pregnant?
- *Nan de kai na! Bobo ga ittsumo kaii chaga!*
  I don't know why! My cunt's always itchy!

Like the other prominent Japanese words for vagina, *bobo* appears around the countryside in different guises. In some villages in the mountains of Yamanashi it pops up as a male organ, but in all other areas *bobo* remains strictly feminine. Yamagata city slang, a renowned melting pot of northern and central Japanese dialects, uses both *bobo* and its local variant *hobo*. In the Niigata province *bebe* is used for vaginas, while *bobo-san* (Ms. Bobo) and *bobo-sama* (Lady Bobo), specify the clitoris. In the Kobe area *bobo* appears as a truncated *bo*. It is only on its home turf, on the island of Kyushu, that *bobo* has over the years absorbed the many different local accents. Just on the streets of Kumamoto it surfaces as *bōbo*, *bōbō*, *bobojo*, and even *bocho*.

The group of *bebe* words is more active and volatile, especially in the north. In Aomori, *bebe* sired *epe* and *epeko*. In Sendai city it mingled with the northern favorite *omanko*, resulting in *obenko*, a word reserved for prepubescent and virginal organs. In the neighboring prefectures of Iwate, Akita, and Yamagata, *bebe* begat *hehe*, which begat *hepe* and *heppe*, which begat *pepe*, which begat *peppe*, which begat *happe*, *bappe*, and *dappe*. (In some areas *dappe* is also a risqué reference to the male organ.)

- *Ore no bebe minē de kun'ro!*
  Don't look at my snatch!

(In standard Japanese, *ore* is a strong, manly word for "I" that only the most masculine women would ever dare use in public. In many northeastern dialects, however, *ore* is considered tough, but completely gender equal.)

- *Sonna mizugi kinde nē zo! Omē no hehe miraretchimau kara!*
  You're not wearing that bathing suit! Your cunt shows through!
- *Omē yō! Or'a hayaku heppe shinē to dame da!*
  Man! If I don't get some cunt soon, I'll go nuts!
- *Omē itsu kara are no peppe mitenē da?*
  When did you get to see her snatch?
- *Omē bappe ni kuriimu tsukene'kka dame da be! Kapakapa da wa!*
  Put some cream on your snatch! It's all dry!

- *Shinjirare'kka yo? Are dappe no ke sotchimatta da be!*
  Man, d'you believe this? She shaved her twat!

Further south, in the province of Ishikawa, *bebe* and *chako* are equally popular, at times fusing into *chabe*, an exclusive regional slang word. About two hundred miles off Ishikawa's coast, on the beautiful and wild islands of Oki, *bebe* is used along with *bebecha*, *bebeko*, and a string of melodious local variants such as *benbe*, *bonbe*, *chanbe*, *chanpe*, and *ochanpe*.

Travelers who follow the development of *bebe* through the mountains of Tohoku, the plains of Kanto, and the tea plantations and rice fields of Chubu gasp when, in Kinki, in the national park of Isseshima, the local in-crowd informs them that they are mistaken, that *bebe* actually means "dirty" or "gross." Only the most unfashionable villagers in outlying coastal areas, they add, might use *bebe* for vagina.

Then, still further south, in Yoshino, near Osaka, *bebe! bebe!* means "potty! potty!" in children's lingo, but "vagina! vagina!" in adult slang. On Tsushima, an island about a hundred miles off the coast of Kyushu, mothers will screech out *bebe!* (yuck!) whenever their toddlers grope about in the mud or splash in roadside puddles. In southern Kyushu, in Kumamoto, Miyazaki, and Kagoshima, the mercurial *bebe* means both "shit" and "female organ."

Another important family of vagina words from central Japan is the *tsubi* group. The *tsubi* terrain stretches from just south of Tokyo, where it appears as *tsūbi*, down to the seaside areas around Hiroshima city. As *tsubi* journeyed south it stayed relatively intact, undergoing few regional sound changes, but in some of the more remote backwaters it has occasionally shifted its meaning. In Shizuoka, on the eel farms of Lake Hamana, *tsubi* has been transformed into both *tsunbi* and the more drawling *tsunbii*, both expressions reserved exclusively for prepubescent organs. On the plains of Mie, *tsubi* and its variant *tsube* have been appropriated as a feisty synonym for clitoris, while just north, in Aichi, *tsubi* refers to intercourse. In villages around Osaka, rough individuals turn the noun *tsubi* into the verb *tsubimagu* (vaginal connection) when coarsely alluding to sex.

Tsubi's southern outpost is the island of Shikoku. In the provinces of Kagawa and Tokushima it precariously shares its turf with *tsube*, which means "anus." To avoid a mixup, many villagers prefer *tsube-nosu* when fast-moving conversations turn to bottoms.

Organs of the Outbacks

As the traveling linguists stalk the various groups of bucolic organs from village to village and town to town, they uncover along the way hardcore aboriginal words exclusive to each region. The remoter the area, the more exotic the words. In the extreme north, in Hokkaido, *pochi, bochi, puchi, mo, m'mo,* and *momo* are of indigenous Ainu background. On Honshu, the main island, the northern province of Akita hides some of the most interesting, if crass, synonyms for vagina. Words for the female organ favored in tougher village circles in Akita are *anbe* (the northern *tanbe* minus the "t"), *nen*, and, down in the area surrounding Akita airport, *betta*.

- *Kyonen no shōgatsu kara ore anbe yatte nē danbe!*
  I didn't get to do any pussy since last New Year's!
- *Ora ni anbe namesasste kunē da.*
  She won't let me lick her twat.
- *Soko no tenugui totte kunro! Betta o nuguwan'nannē.*
  Gimme that towel there! I wanna dry my snatch.

Just south, by the ski slopes of Yamagata, local thugs enjoy using words like *biren*, *choko*, and *chame*, while in the rice-field area in the southern part of the province racy farmers use *abecho* or *apecho* to distinguish virginal organs, and *satōbako* (sugar box) for those more experienced. One province over, in the bay of Sendai, the halibut and tuna fishermen use *berako*, a type of hogfish, to allude to young organs.

One of the roughest village expressions, stumbled upon in the mountains of Aizu, is *kumananna* (bear's hole), also pronounced *kuma ana* (bear hole). Village men use it primarily as a jocular synonym for vagina, but also as a blunt way to describe women.

- *Ore kon'ēda are no kumananna midakeyo!*
  Man, I got to see her puntang!
- *Ore ga kēte kitara yō, ano onna kuma ana aratte toko dabe sa! Ora tamage da!*
  When I got back, that woman was washing her twat! Man, what a turn on!
- *Kondo Tōkyō kara kita kuma ana ii onna da bē gā!*
  That bit-of-ass just in from Tokyo, she's one good looking woman!
- *Areya nisa no kumananna ga?*
  Is that there your bit-of-ass?

An interesting set of off-color words in the province of Niigata is of chaste Buddhist lineage. *Daibutsu* (Great Buddha) is used throughout the nation as a naughty euphemism for penis, the Buddha's shaved crown suggesting a sacrilegious resemblance to the bloated head of an erect organ. *Bōzu* (priest) is another popular penile alternative based on the shaved-head association.

Religious words for the female organ, however, are more rare. In certain Niigata circles *nyorai-sama* (Lord Buddha), is the vagina; by entering the world of the Buddha the worshipper will be transported to ecstasy. For an even stronger touch of profanity, some individuals opt for *rurikō nyorai* (Lapis-lazuli Buddha).

Kannon-sama (Goddess of Mercy) is another popular regional word. *Kannon*, whose name literally means "she who hears their cries (of anguish)," has the added attraction that she is a Bodhisattva—she postpones her own ascent to nirvana so that she can guide men to joy. Some groups use *kannon-sama* to refer to the clitoris. Even the Buddhist temples have not survived Niigata street slang unscathed. *Okunoin* (inner sanctuary) is used as a zesty reference to the vagina, while *honzon no kageishi*, the hidden image of the Holy Buddha, serves blasphemously as the clitoris.

Further down the road, the prefecture of Tochigi offers the unique *fune*. Some villagers argue that its etymology is *fune*, as in "boat." Others, however, point out that since most of the mountain villagers who enjoy using the term have never seen a boat, the original inspiration must have been *fu ne* (couple sleep).

On the coasts of Mie, in the area of the old pearl fisheries of Shima, the private local words for vagina are *konbo* and the harsher *hamehame* (jab jab). In the southern part of Honshu, in the precincts of the Setonaikai National Park in Yamaguchi, the favorite regional word is *bonshii*, while across the straits of Iyo on the island of Shikoku, unusual words like *chobo*, *magu*, *okai*, and *okaisu* are heard in the impenetrable dialect of the local roughs.

The most bizarre words for vagina in Japan are to be found in the ancient Kingdom of Ryūkū, today's Okinawa. Our linguists board ship at Kagoshima on Kyushu, and island-hop through the hundred-odd islands that comprise Okinawa, interrogating locals in the fishing ports all the way to Yonagunijima, off the coast of Taiwan. In their ports of call they encounter exotic languages, unintelligible from one island to the next.

Before their boat leaves Kagoshima harbor, the travelers have a last chance to pick up a few final indelicate expressions from the dock: *ohako* (box), *mame* (bean), *mochi* (rice cake), and *bocho*, all synonyms for mature organs, while *anabachi* (new pot) is reserved for virgins. One of the favorite harbor-slang words in Kagoshima is *manzu*, the local pronunciation of *manjū* (bean-jam bun). An unsolved linguistic mystery to this day is that this bun also makes a cameo appearance on distant Ishigaki island, almost six hundred miles out to sea, where *manjō* is the female organ, and *manjō shin* (doing bean bun), means "raunchy intercourse."

The most widespread Okinawan words for vagina are *hi*, *hii*, *pi* and *pii* (which, to the travelers' surprise, also mean "fart" on most of the islands). Other general words popular on the islands are *hō*, *haji*, and the polite and circumspect *mē*, which in actual fact means "front." The inhabitants of the tiny islet of Kuroshima use *kizaku* (shell) in their harsh local slang, while further out, on the island of Tokunoshima, the local taboo words are *homa* and *to*. Nearer to the main island of Okinawa, on minuscule Yoronjima, the island words for vagina are *po* and *pūo*.

On Okinawa proper the most common rough word for the organ is *hōmi*. Tourists are often startled to see it scrawled on the walls of public toilets with the elegant characters *hō* for "jewel" and *mi* for "taste." The fiercest Okinawa expression for sex is *hōmi yari* (doing tasty jewels). In the jargon of the local mobsters, who are known as *ashibjā* (the men about town) in the capital city of Naha, *hōmi yari* has a sterner meaning: it refers to gangbangs and forced rape.

In the Okinawan countryside the dialects change from valley to valley. As one drives north out of Naha city on Route 58, the rurals' "h" becomes more and more like "p." *Hōmi* gradually changes into *homi*, and then as one passes the U.S. airbase at Kadena, into *homi*, *hhomi*, and then *bhomi*, *bomi*, and *phomi*. By the time one reaches the extreme northern part of the island, with its rugged hills and dreamy fishing villages, the southern *hōmi* has changed into *pomi*.

The next port of linguistic interest is Miyako, a flat pleasant island about ten hours by boat from Okinawa. In the harbor of Hirara (population 50,000) the dock crowd use *ujanma*, while the inhabitants of the town of Gusukube, on the southeastern side of the island, prefer their own exclusive word, *pssi*.

The southernmost outpost of Japan's empire, and the end of the travelers' linguistic journey, is the isolated archipelago of Yaeyama. Weather permitting, the ferry from Okinawa makes its way over the two hundred sixty miles of sea only once a week. One of the larger and wilder islands of the group is Iriomote, whose mountains and tropical rainforests separate its two towns, Ohara and Funaura. In Iriomote beach slang, the words for the female organ are *gutchu* (dug out) and *gira* (shell), pronounced by some as a heftier, drawn-out *giiira*. On Kohama, a tiny island off Iriomote's coast, the hardcore local words are *mitoma* and *piishii*.

The most remote of the Yaeyama islands is Yonagunijima, whose two thousand-odd inhabitants speak an exotic dialect they call the Dunan language, known in the region for its long, tongue-twisted words. A virginal organ, for instance, is *bingasanuminuka'agami*, while an aroused female organ is described as *minukagaranderuchiru*. The fashionable crowd on the island enjoy bouncing foreign expressions (that is, expressions from nearby islands) about in their speech. Favorites are the general Okinawan word *hi* and the Yaeyama word *piishii*.

A few decades ago Yanagita Kunio, the renowned father of Japanese folklore, went on a similar word mission through Japan, one that took him over rugged mountains and through perilous valleys. His interest, however, was in snails. As he left Kyoto, the old capital, snails turned from *dedemushi* to *maimai* to *katatsumuri* to *tsuburi*. To Yanagita's surprise, the further afield he roamed, the older the words for snail became.

The distribution of words for the female organ, however, was much more spirited than that of the snail. Throughout the Middle Ages small sailing vessels transported these words from port to port, all the way from Hokkaido in the northeast to Kyushu in the southwest, and from Kyushu to the Kingdom of Okinawa, to the southernmost tip of Japan. At every stop thousands of *funajorō* (ship prostitutes) lay in wait, ready to barter risqué local words.

7 ▪ Sushi Slang

ONE OF the brightest and most challenging forms of Japanese slang is spoken down by the port in the wholesale fish markets of large cities in the dark hours before dawn. By 4:00 in the morning gigantic markets like Tokyo's Tsukiji, Osaka's Kuromon, and Hakata's Yanagibashi are churning with action. Thousands of fish stalls have been set up and box carts, fish wheelbarrows, vans, trucks, and huge sixteen-wheelers jam the streets and alleys. By 4:30 the city's top sushi chefs arrive with their drivers, and crowds of bustling fish brokers, auctioneers, wholesalers, and traders eye the catch and chatter in loud *besshari* (an inversion of *shaberi*, "talk"), the earthy market slang.

These early morning markets, known in vendor jargon as *seriichi* (competition markets) and *ichiasa* (from *asaichi*, "morning fair"), are hotbeds of linguistic creativity. While the city sleeps, thousands of exotic slang words surge through the stalls as tons of fish exchange hands, millions of yen flow from one pocket to another, and chefs whose reputations are at stake fight each other tooth and nail for the best fish at the best price. By 5:00 the auctioneers—*tankashi* (curse masters)—launch into their loud *tataki* (banging), the hard sales drives that artfully pitch the retailers against each other.

To these specialists a mackerel is not simply a mackerel, nor is a chunk of tuna just tuna. Ask a wholesaler for the Japanese term for herring, and swarms of non-dictionary words come pouring out: *berotsuke, nishio, miyaki, segai, kado, chongo, kōraiiwashi*. A herring can be *kaku* (horn) if its head is particularly pointed, *kakutobi* (flying horn) if it has a well-developed, athletic body, *ōba* (large wing) if its fin is eye-catching, or *koha* (small wing) if it is not. The healthiest, most expensive herring are discreetly referred to as *tobiuo* (flying fish); *nakatobi* (inside fliers) are herring of medium interest, and the smallest of the batch are *haitobi* (rope fliers). *Tōnishin* is a herring that has been caught in deep ocean waters out of season. Watanabe Shigeru, in his 1955 book *Hokkaido Hōgenshū*, identifies *tōnishin* as a Hokkaido dialect word. *Tō*, he claims, is an Ainu term for swamp that was added to *nishin*, the standard Japanese word for herring. A herring that is sold after its treasured roe has been pressed out is *tsubunishi*.

Even more words tumble across the fish stall counters when the vendor is asked about dried herring. A popular southern word is *hanishi*, while *kachanishi, sakkaranishi*, and *nishipa* migrated down from northern Honshu and Hokkaido. If herring have been both dried and cut they are called *hokawari, somenishi, teppira*, or *sasakinishi*.

When a wholesaler manages to hawk a whole consignment of herring, surprised colleagues describe him as doing *kakubei*. The only term for herring that never seems to appear in private market talk however is *nishin*, the word used by everyone else in Japan.

The biggest and most famous fish market in all of Japan is Tokyo's Tsukiji, which locals lovingly refer to as *Tōkyō no daidokoro* (Tokyo's kitchen). This market has been the single largest mover-and-shaker of modern Japanese slang. Year in year out, Tokyo's toughest hard-selling and hard-buying individuals match their wits in early-morning auction halls, in wholesale depots, behind fish tanks, and in market aisles. New words travel fast.

A woman driving a sixteen-wheeler might, for instance, say in jest that she has no patience with what she calls *pōraroido boizu* (Polaroid boys): when you press their button in bed there is a big flash and the fun is over. A fish-box carrier, known in market slang as *karuko* (light child), might call someone *furufēsu*, (full face)—the sprightly implication being that the individual's face extends all the way to the back of his head (i.e., he's completely bald). A nearby wholesaler hears the inspired neologisms and cheerily passes them on to a retailer, who passes them on to a sushi chef. The sushi chef gives the expressions a debonair public send-off by weaving them into over-the-counter anecdotes. Businessmen, secretaries, students, and car mechanics, having enjoyed their fresh Tsukiji market tuna at the sushi counter, bow, thank the chef, and take the new words home.

Tsukiji has been the driving force behind Tokyo's slang scene since the disastrous 1923 earthquake, when the wholesale fish market fled from Nihonbashi to Shiba, and then in 1932 settled in its present location on the banks of the Sumida river by the port. The nearby freight depot in Shiodome (Japan's first train station, built in 1872), the closeness of the port, and the arrival of the Hibiya subway line in 1964, all gave

Tsukiji its unshakable position as Tokyo's most important linguistic crossroads.

Tsukiji had become even more important when Tokyo's wholesale vegetable market set up nearby, in the area that the old guard still calls *jōgai* (the place outside). A heated linguistic rivalry began between the two sister markets as the fish crowd, their turf invaded, jealously stepped up their slangy *besshari*, while the willful grocers energetically cultivated what they called their *fuchō* (the inversion of *chōfu*, "code language"). If the fish crowd could give their sardines magnetic names such as *aoko*, *nagashi*, *komamono*, *hirago*, *tare*, *koshinaga*, *gomoku*, *donpo*, *karagaki*, *kigama*, *shikoro*, *yasura*, or the Korean *chongori*, then the farm crowd was not about to lag behind. Along with their fruit and vegetables, farmers imported captivating words from faraway provinces. A commonplace squash, for instance (*kabocha* in standard Japanese) could be glamorized with a host of cryptic market words like *abura-shime* (oil press), *kinka* (golden melon), *kintōka* (golden winter melon), *nanka* (southern melon), *yūgao* (gourd), and *satsuma yūgao* (gourd from Satsuma), *satsuma uri* (melon from Satsuma), or just *satsuma* and *osatsu* for short. Squash words from the south became especially popular. *Bonka* came up from the Mie region, *bōbura* from Osaka, *bōta* from Shimane, *tōgan* from Hiroshima, and *obora* and *onzo* from the province of Kagawa on Shikoku island. The most intriguing batch of squash words, however, are older terms that were the rage in market stalls in the fifties and sixties. They establish a Korean squash connection with jargonistic names like *karauri* (Korean melon), *karayūgao* (Korean gourd), *chōsen* (the politically incorrect name for Korea popular during the Japanese occupation), and its more elegant version *ochōsen* (the honorific *"o"* and *Chōsen*, "Korea"). Market vendors, baffled as to why these words were turning up in market slang, could only conjecture that the vegetables must have been originally imported *en masse* from Korea.

At a Fish Auction

The market jumps to full action at 5:20 A.M. sharp. A bell tinkles, and there is a stampede of rubber boots over the sloshy cement floor as buyers of every shape and size dodge haulers, carts, and wheelbarrows, racing each other to reach the platform by the gigantic metal fish tanks. When there is a particularly large rush of retailers, such as during festivals or before the New Year, the delighted auctioneers exclaim:

- *Oi! Ojime kuru zo!*
  Yo! A big push is coming!

  Or more playfully:

- *Ki o tsuke! Janjan da!*
  Get ready, it's ding dong!

The buyers charging toward the auction platform are called *zabu*, a name that, according to the market crowd, was inspired by *zabuzabu* (splish splash), the sound of their feet racing through bilgy puddles. The first fish to be hawked at the market, at 5:20, are alive, swimming large and small in their tanks. At 5:30 there is a second rush as the auctioning of boxes of fresh fish packed on ice begins on another level. Then, within minutes, the whole market is agog. Bells peal, loudspeakers bellow, and sirens blare as sales start up all over the building: the night's catch on the first floor, fresh tuna at ground level, sea urchins and oysters by the fish tanks, and rows upon rows of frozen tuna outside by the docks.

At these auctions only the slickest survive. Selling fish wholesale is called *otosu* (throwing), and buying wholesale is *mukaeru* (welcoming). Day in day out, the same hardline professionals bid against each other with deft maneuvers and slippery bluffs. Newcomers, known as *ichigen* (once seen), do not stand much of a chance. Before they need apply for a license they have to be fluent in the market's *besshari* and study the auctioneers' sales methods, known as *hōgaku* (direction). They have to learn the many little secret hand signals that can mean anything from "yes please, I'll have that large fish over there", to "at that price, forget it!" The single hardest task for the newcomer is decoding what is known as *tankabai* (curse sale) or *tontonbai* (bang bang sale). This is the impenetrable, droning chant of the auctioneer as he plays on the secret winks and hand gestures of the buying crowd.

Experience has made the bidding retailers distrustful. They have spent the pre-dawn hours peeking into tanks and into *danbe*, the boxes where fresh fish lie on ice. They sniff and eye their favorite fish, tapping their gills, looking deep into their eyes, and glaring at fins and tails. No retailer wants to be caught buying an *aotan* (bruise), a fish that on closer inspection has gone slightly fusty. The gigantic frozen tuna that lie in rows all the way down to the dock are checked by what is called *shippo o kiru* (cut the tail). The retailers walk from fish to fish flicking their fingers on the skin to evaluate its oiliness, and studying the lines on the exposed meat with flashlights. If blood oozes out in blobs, the technical market term is *azuki ga demasu*, "azuki beans are seeping out." If a tuna turns out to be wanting, it is labeled *dabo*, an insulting cognomen that came from *dabohaze* (goby) an unattractive, spiny-finned little fish.

The catch of the night is kept fresh in styrofoam boxes that market slang calls *taibako*. A perfectly packed box of herring or mackerel contains twenty-one fish piled in neat tiers, and is called *hitochobo* (dice throw); if you count up all the little dots on a cube they add up to twenty-one. Some market packers will then top up the box with water and ice cubes (a process known as *suihyō*, "water ice"), while others aim for a crisper fish by skipping the water and just packing the fish down with crushed ice (a process known as *jōhyō*, "top ice"). Of all the retailers, those bidding for live fish from the tanks are the wariest. The careful professional asks himself: How alert is that fish over there? How energetic? Does it swim about briskly enough? After all, even the peppiest specimen might well be *aniki* (brother), an elderly fish. If in doubt, the bidder mutters *su ga itta*, "the nest went," and walks off.

The biggest scandal occurs when a fish dies before everyone's eyes while it is being auctioned. In such calamitous cases the bewildered auctioneer turns to his audience and utters the Buddhist death euphemism:

- *Agatta!*
Its soul has risen!

The auction does not always run smoothly. There is often ill-feeling when one bidder outmaneuvers another and manages to get his hands on a prize specimen. The derailed retailer will furiously describe his predicament as *naki* (crying).

A more serious problem is when two arch-rivals, battling each other for a fish, arrive at a bidding impasse known as *tsuki* (together). The men first bark at each other in heated *besshari* while the auctioneer and the other retailers wait impatiently. If neither of the two will back down, they do a quick *jan ken pon* (paper-scissors-rock game), and the winner takes the fish. In some rare cases, however, opponents will lunge at each other in what is known in the market as *juzu* (Buddhist rosary). Punches fly, other retailers take sides, the auctioneers join in, and the market police come rushing to the scene.

As the pre-dawn auctions draw to a close the bidders race off to their fish stalls. In the Tsukiji market some sixteen hundred stalls clutter around the central shipping platform, known as Shiomachijaya (tea house for the awaiting of the turning tide).

To the vendor, his market spot is his *niwaba* (garden place). The most strategic stall sites are called *tenshoba* (heavenly spots). The market commission holds lotteries for locations every three years, but there is still ill-feeling among vendors about who stands where.

As the stalls open, lines of regular clients are waiting impatiently with bundles of yen notes in hand, and the vendors begin hacking away at the fish with their heavy *deba bōchō* cleavers. Every slash of the blade has its *besshari* name: *saku* (sever) means slicing the fish in half through the center bone, *daimyō oroshi suru* (doing a feudal lord drop) means cutting a fish in half by pressing in the knife point above the gills and cutting towards the tail, *sanmai oroshi suru* (doing a three-piece drop) means cleaving the fish in half through its bone and then slicing it in half again from side to side.

The early customers study the fish greedily, pointing and winking at their favorite specimens, trying to get in their bids for the best chunks. During these first crucial minutes every fish and every fish part is soused with hundreds of market names. A robust tuna is called *kuronbo* (black boy), *gotatsuke* (troublemaker), *ōuo* (big fish), *ōshibi* (big tuna), *seinaga* (height long), and *ōtaro* (big Taro). *Yotsu* ("four," as in forty kilograms) is the run-of-the-mill eighty-pounder. The *metsuke* (overseer), *meguro* (black eye), and *mejika* (doe) are the daintier, younger tuna.

Every inch of fish has its *besshari* name. The large blocks of tuna laid out ready for sale are called *dote* (mud embankments), and the anxious retailers and chefs count these fish blocks in *chō*: *itchō* (one block), *nichō* (two blocks), *sanchō* (three blocks).

- *Ano gotatsuke no itchō! Yoroshiku, na!*
  One block of troublemaker! Please take care of me! (Gimme a chunk from that humongous tuna over there! A nice chunk, OK?)
- *Kono nichō ikura kai?*
  How much d'ya want for both chunks?
- *Sanchō to waribiki suru yo!*
  Take all three blocks and I'll give 'em to you cheap!

Haranimai (two sheets of belly) is the highly prized stomach, which is served up caked in salt as an exotic delicacy from the northern province of Iwate. The head of the fish is called *kama*, the top section including the gills *kami*, and the bottom part is *shimo*. *Engawa* (porch) is a fin.

The uninitiated shopper at the market might be quite surprised to hear a sushi chef say, "What a beautiful porch! I'll take it, and wrap up those embankments over there for me too."

As the market words narrow down to the more specific parts of a fish they cross into sushi bar territory, where they are used by customers with delicate palates to order raw slices from particular areas of a fish. *Ōtoro* (big fatty-tuna) is the expensive meat carved out of the frontal underbelly, *chūtoro* (medium fatty-tuna) are slices of underbelly from further down, *nakaochi* (inside dividend) is the meat around the backbone, and *akami* (red taste) is the cheap reddish meat from the lean area near the tail.

Discriminating sushi bar clients will pay $100 and more for a portion of sushi with a strip of the best Tsukiji tuna. As a result, tensions mount when one rival chef manages to snap up a chunk of fish that another had been eyeing. A sushi chef is only as good as the tuna he manages to get hold of, so when he loses out the word used is *naku* (crying), the same expression that vendors use when they are outsmarted at the early morning auction. As a foiled chef might complain:

- *Kesa sandai me naita!*
  It's the third time I'm crying this morning!
  (It's the third piece of fish that was snatched from under my nose!)

- *Dōshite sonna ni nakisaseta!*
  I can't believe you're making me cry like this!
  (How could you have let him get that piece I wanted?)

When tempers flare and irate chefs fly at each other's throats, the market *besshari* word is *deiri* (entrance and exit).

The earliest customers at the fish stall are also the toughest. Sushi chefs and local Tokyo retailers pride themselves on their *irime* (false eye), their uncanny ability to judge the weight of a fish to a gram. As a result, many buyers and vendors who have longstanding relationships avoid using scales so as not to offend the others' sensibilities. Vendors who are particularly fond of a customer will even go as far as playing *kakedashi* (novice); the vendor packs a chunk of fish, ostentatiously misjudging its weight as only a beginner would, letting the favored buyer get away with a few extra grams. On slow days during tea breaks some fish stalls even do a bit of illegal *chikamedori* (close-up eye take), in which a small friendly market group dumps yen notes onto the stall counter, gambling on the exact weight of a fish. The trick is to assess how much water might have seeped into it while it was floating in the *danbe* among the ice cubes.

After the best of the catch has been sold within the first minutes, the vendors prepare themselves to face the rush of local fishmongers, lesser chefs, and tough Tokyo matrons who have large families to feed. These customers are classified as *jinkyaku* (the inversion of *kyakujin*, "patron"). If there is a lull after the first wave of customers, the wary vendor defines the situation as:

- *E ni kaita jishin.*
  Confidence painted in a picture.

The implication is that he is putting on a brave face even though his confidence is somewhat diaphanous. If the lull is unnervingly long the situation becomes *bōzu* (priest), the apprehensive pun being that the customers are as few as the hairs on a priest's carefully shaven head. The worried vendor might call out to a neighboring stall:

- *Omē mo kyō bōzu kai?*
  Are you also a priest today?

But in the big wholesale market, business is always brisk and the sellers barely have time to figure out whom to serve next. When crowds line up in front of a stall the market word is *jindachi* (men stand). When there are more clients than a vendor can handle he will yell, *jin ga shimateru* (men are strangling). When stalls are completely mobbed by haggling crowds the vendor and his assistants gasp:

- *Tsukkomu!*
  We're being rammed!

Vendors are never too busy to find the right *besshari* word to describe a particular customer, and over the years market slang has amassed a rich stockpile of terms. The most creative, if unkind, *besshari* words are reserved for the women who come to the market.

Female customers who are master hagglers are called *hangaku* (half pricers) or *hikizuri* (draggers). Those with a knack for wrestling fish cheaply from a confused vendor during a rush are called *chochoji* and *omatsu* (those who wait). Gullible women who blindly buy whatever the vendor puts in front of them are the *bakabatsu*.

Some of the cruelest *besshari* words playfully distinguish a customer's salient features. *Ōtara* (large cod) is a hefty, somewhat alarming matron, *hattojiri* (startle bottom) is one with a startlingly large bottom, and *fukure* (swollen) is a jolly woman with fat, round cheeks. *Botamochi*, the tasty rice-cake dumpling covered in bean jam, refers to women with flat, dumpling-like faces. *Daburu bikkuri* (double shock) are women who, as they approach the stall, look so attractive that the vendor has a shock, but when they arrive at the counter the vendor has a second shock as the scales fall from his eyes.

The most typical early morning matrons, vendors say, are *yamabushi* (mountain priest) and *daibutsuzoku* (the colossal Buddha gang). The mountain priest is the housewife who has tried, with disastrous results, to save her elaborate hairstyle of the night before. The colossal Buddha gang are more practical: they run from stall to stall, with their hair still tightly wrapped in rollers, their heads reminiscent of the ringlets on the great statue of the Buddha at Nara.

8 ▪ Gambling Japanese

WHEN TOUGH Japanese gamblers meet in the smoky and illegal back rooms of their local betting parlors, they speak an elegant slang that becomes swifter and more labyrinthine as bundle after bundle of yen notes slam onto the table. Cards, dice, hand movements, tricks, stunts, dodges, and stratagems all have special names that often go back to medieval times, when gangs of heroic gamblers marauded their way up and down the countryside. These were glamorous men known as *bakuto*, and legend has it that they stole from the rich, gave to the poor, did knightly deeds, and spoke their own cryptic lingo that no one else could understand. They defended their honor and their right to gamble with swords that, in those days, only samurai were allowed to carry.

The *bakuto* of the nineties still work in groups—gangster groups—and call themselves *kage* (shadows), *kashimoto* (financiers), *buchishi* (bang masters) and *bakuchikoki* (betting tumblers). During the day they make an illegal living by quietly running roulettes, poker halls, high-tech slot machine parlors, and betting associations that deal in illegal wagers on sumo wrestling and baseball. At night, however, they aim to bolster their income in private all-professional parlors known as *bon* (trays), *iremono* (receptacles), and more furtively *ageita* (trap doors).

The high-stake games that these tough men play are known as *oshikai* (push buying), and when pros play against pros the match is known as *aitsuki* (the inversion of *tsukiai*, "meeting"). In these heated encounters, the gamblers play traditional Japanese games. In *tōsen*, for instance, a vase or statue is set up as a target. Yen notes are leafed down onto a tray, the burly gangsters line up against the wall, and exquisite fans with beautiful classical nature motifs swish open. The men take a deep breath, and there is a colorful flurry as the fans hurtle through the air. The fan whose heel lands closest to the target wins.

A less athletic game is *hanafuda* (flower cards). Here the mobsters sit sedately around a large cushion and deal out a deck of forty-eight picture cards showing blossom branches, shrubs, flowers, trees, animals, and red ribbons of *tanzaku*—dainty traditional scrolls with poems.

The cards are divided into sets of four, one set for every month. The January set is called *matsu* (pine). On the first card, a crane looks up at the moon against a backdrop of pines. Then comes a poetry card with a subdued seasonal poem, followed by more pines, which, the gamblers explain, are ancient symbols of good fortune. The four February cards are called *ume* (plum), and show nightingales, plum blossoms, and more poetry. The March cards are called *sakura* (cherry blossoms): the cherry trees are in full bloom, and striped curtains hang from branches hiding blossom watchers.

The game is elegant. Its history stretches back to

the Heian period (794–1185 A.D.), when the refined ladies and gentlemen of the Imperial Court played *kachō awase* (matching flowers and birds). But with large fortunes at stake, the gamblers inevitably eye each other warily. A new pack is opened every session, for few can resist the tempting urge to do "chicken" (*chikin*, from *chiki-in*, a playful parlor inversion of *inchiki*, "trickery"). Card-fiddling methods are collectively called *goto*, which is short for *shigoto* (work). A habitual swindler, should he survive the wrath of his peers, is known as *gotoshi* (work master). When a pro smells perfidy in the air, he will quietly mutter to himself *zuku* or *zuiteru* (as in *kanzuiteru*, "I scent a plot").

- *Ki o tsukero yo! Aitsu ni zukareru to mazui ze!*
  Careful! If he catches on, we're in for it!
- *Sono heya ni haitta totan, zuita yo.*
  The moment I walked into that room I smelt something fishy.

The untrusting player will glare at his opponent's hand, wondering if the flower cards have been *aori* (fanned) or *irotsuki* (stained).

- *Mo aitsura to wa nido to yaru mon ka, aori wa kori gori da ze!*
  I'm never playing with those guys again, there's nothing but cheating!
- *Konna ni makeru nante hen da ze, irotsuki ni chigainē!*
  I mean, to keep on losing like that, the decks must have been stacked!

One typical trick is *dosa*, a word borrowed from

pickpocketing slang. A player with an exceptionally bad hand will flick a compromising card up his sleeve and quickly substitute a more favorable one.

Another classical trick is *okei*. The trickster befriends the *chūban* (middle number), a junior mobster who does all the odd jobs at the gambling parlor. The friendly *chūban* leaves oily hors d'ouevre plates strategically lying about so that the player can catch reflections of his partners' hands. In his 1986 book *Jisho ni Nai Kotoba*, Yoshizaki Junji claims that the word *okei* was invented in commemoration of Madame Okei, a malicious medieval heroine featured in the old theatrical hit *Kana Tehon Chūshingura*.

The *hanafuda* players gather around the pillow on the floor, and the round, or *bushō* (from *shōbu*, "match") begins. The cards are smaller, stiffer, and much thicker than a Western deck. The shuffler holds the pack in one hand, and quickly pulls out small clutches of cards with the other from the bottom of the deck, slipping them on top.

In professional games, the shuffler is called *biki*. He shuffles (*mazeru*) and passes the cards to the cutter (*doni*) who cuts the deck and passes it to the dealer, the *oya* (daddy). The players pick up their cards and the game begins. The gambling slang words for playing a round are *bushōneru* (from *shōbu*, "match" added to the verb-ending *neru*) and its shortened version, *buneru*. As the tension mounts, the hard cards slap onto the pillow. Every player tries to do *kanban* (poster), what Western card circles call bluffing. Those who are desperate even resort to *shamisen*, prattling loudly while the opponent tries to figure out his next move. Forlorn mobsters who have been dealt a singularly bad hand might go so far as doing *bankiri* (evening cut). In a rage, they capsize the card pillow and lunge at a nearby opponent, shouting:

- *Damashi yagatta na! Ore wa kono me de hakkiri to mita ze!*
  He fucking cheated! I saw it with my own eyes!

When a game is lost, the unlucky players are pronounced *buchidao*, from *buchi* (hit) and *taoreta* (toppled). An even more jocular word for a lost game is *banzai* (hurrah). When screaming *banzai* at a baseball match or in a football stadium, one usually throws one's arms up in ecstasy. The losers of the *hanafuda* game also throw their arms up—but they do so in agony over all the cash they have lost. The money that ends up in the winner's tray is called *ochizeze*, a humorous dialect version of *ochi zeni* (dropped cash), and the cut that goes to the illegal parlor is the *terasen* (temple coin).

- *Kyō no ochizeze wa nakanaka na mon' da ze.*
  Man, today's winnings are pretty good.
- *Temēra terasen ireru no wasurenna'yo!*
  Yo! Don't forget to drop your temple donations in there!

If a match turns out to be a draw, the opponents declare it *bushōnashi* (from *shōbunashi*, "no match"), and the colorful cards are dealt out again.

- *Konkai wa bushōnashi kā. Mo ippen yarō ze!*
  So it's an even match. Lets go for another round!

The winner of the first round is *hatsu uke* (first receiver). The gambler who wins round after round is named *uketsubo* (receiving pot). The powerful gambling bosses, *ōrin* (large wheels), will often invite important business associates, even politicians, to the game and make ostentatious mistakes known as *kezuri* (deletions) and *kaimachi* (the inversion of *machigai*, "error"). This is a genial underworld way of obliging influential friends with large sums of money without actually bribing them.

Dice Throwers

Gamblers interested in a faster game with quick cash prizes play dice. They are a tougher, earthier mob, which is shunned by refined cliques. Gambling slang calls them *hoira*, *baicha*, *sēmi*, and *kyokamuzabucha*, all Korean words from Japan's ethnically diverse gangster scene. The jargon these men speak in their parlors is mottled with Korean slang words; amateurs are called *chinoniruta* and *chiroriruta*, and pro gamblers new at a certain dice game are called *kyōkan*. *Karikugi* or *hihicha* is "gambling," *karichun* "swindling," and guns are given Korean names like *tai* (sleep), *tējitari* (pork chop), and *buchitani* (handgun).

- *Kyō wa karikugi ni tējitari wasurennayo.*
  Don't forget to take your gun along to today's match.
- *Karichun ga ore ni kiku to demo omotteru no ka nē? Ore wa chiroriruta ja nē ze!*

He thinks he can just fuck me over like that? I'm no beginner you know!

The most popular dice game over the years has been *chōhan* (odd-even). The dice throwing croupier (*tsubofuri*) shouts:

- *Chō ka? Han ka?*
  Will it be odds? Or evens?

The nervous players dally, waiting for what dice slang calls *tsukeme*, a flash of clairvoyance that will ensure the jackpot. The bets are placed, and the dice are popped into what some parlors call *tsubo* (pot) and other parlors call *bon* (tray). Some less fastidious clubs prefer *nagesai*, (throw dice), in which the croupier shakes the dice directly in his hand. The dice are briskly joggled, the clients hold their breath, and the croupier does what Japanese slang calls *kokashi* (a drop)—he lets the dice roll.

The dice are called *saikoro* (bone seed), or just *sai* for short, in remembrance of ancient times when they were first imported from China as little bits of bone. Gamblers also call their dice *kotsu* (bone), *chobo* (dots), and *ichiroku* (one-six), while the dots on the dice are called *sai no me*, or *kotsu no me* (eyes of the bone).

- *Sono sai no me wa ore ni totcha yoku nē na.*
  Those dots on the dice never come right to me.
- *Chikushō, me ga kasunde kite, kotsu no me ga yoku mie ya shinē!*
  Shit, I'm getting so short-sighted I can't see these dots!

The greatest fear of the Japanese dice addict is loaded dice, and modern high-stake gamblers demand electromagnetic checks before staking as much as a yen. Some careful aficionados even bring along state-of-the-art homing devices. A bogus die is called *akusai* (evil bone), or *ikasamasai* (swindling bone), and the minute lead weight that makes it tilt to a winning number is called *omori* (plummet). Some gambling circles also refer to these dice as *ittenmono* (same-dot piece): however often you throw the dice, they always tumble onto the same number.

Other terms for bogus dice are *nanabu* (seven parts), *dōgu* ("tools," as in tools of the trade), *dara*, and *temoku*. The quintessential trick, pros explain, is to start off with bona fide dice. Play a few rounds, lose a few games, let the stakes climb, and then do a quick *saikorogui* (dice gobble) where you snatch up the respectable dice and quickly slip in the fraudulent ones.

Over the years, the swindlers, known as *ineshi*, have come up with the most outlandish tricks. One of the droller stratagems was called *anaguma* (bear in the hole). The bear, in this case, is a burly crook who sits hidden in a "hole" under the gambling board. Using magnets, strings, and even high-tech remote control devices, he secretly ensures that a parlor's fortunes remain promising.

These con artists have traditionally been known as *ame* (sweet) because of the mellifluous speech that hooks the unsuspecting, and goads them on to betting ever higher amounts. To keep the atmosphere congenial, the swindlers would surround themselves with a crowd of pleasant counterfeit customers, friends of the parlor, who would pose as high-rolling winners, landing one jackpot after the other. These shills were known as *tsuko* (handles) and *kuchihari* (mouth stretchers). Some circles also called them *sakura* (cherry blossoms) because they were always suave individuals in attractive clothes, and people would come in throngs to see them win.

The *chōhan* dice game developed in the late Edo period (1600–1867), and has managed to flourish despite constant government persecution. In the early years, professional gamblers were carted off in chains and punished with tattoos that marked them as criminals. In Osaka they were branded with two fat horizontal stripes just above the elbow, and in Tokyo with two stripes just above the wrist.

The real reign of terror, however, began in the first year of Meiji, 1868, when the new administration passed a series of lethal anti-gambling laws in a radical attempt to bring Japan on a par with the West. The buying and selling of dice was strictly prohibited, and rows upon rows of fair-ground gambling stalls were pulled down throughout the country and their owners thrown in jail. Masukawa Kōichi, in his 1989 book *Tobaku no Nihon Shi*, writes that repeat offenders were even decapitated, their heads displayed in public as a warning.

But throughout the country the dice rolled on. Desperate gamblers went further underground, formed tighter cliques, were reduced to carving their own dice, and invented new top-secret words. There was a flood of new dice games. Some cliques played *ōme shōme* (big-eye small-eye), where those shouting *ōme* (big eye) had to get numbers four to six in order to win, and those shouting *shōme* (small eye), numbers one to three. Others played the simple *pin korogashi* (number 1 rolls): pop the die into the *tsubo* (container), shake it, and let it roll, and if number one comes up, you win. Every clique specialized in different games. *Tensai* (heavenly bones) was played with five dice, *kitsune* (fox) with three, *itten jiroku* (one–heaven six–earth) with two, *chobo ichi* (one cube) with one.

The most striking feature of the secret slangs that developed in the dark, illegal parlors of fin-de-siècle Japan were the different counters with which gamblers tallied the dice dots. Southern dice slang, for instance, invented:

1—*pin*	6—*rotsu*
2—*nizo*	7—*un*
3—*san*	8—*chō*
4—*ya*	9—*kabu*
5—*goke*	10—*buta*

Northern dice throwers developed their own variation:

1—*pin*	6—*pō*
2—*o*	7—*ya*
3—*zun*	8—*hai*
4—*ya*	9—*kabu*
5—*goke*	10—*buta*

In the more elaborate three-dice games, the dice throwers fabricated more sophisticated names that were adopted into parlor slang as private puns and witticisms. When the dice fell into a 2–1–2 combination, the gamblers would shout *otomo* (attendant), and when they fell into 2–5–2, *nikkō* (sunlight). A 5–5–5 score was dubbed *ōkami no ashi* (wolf's foot), and 1–1–1, *mikkabōzu* (three-day priest). But some of the counters were given gaucher names. Whenever, for instance, the dice came up as 4–5–4, the crowd would break into peals of laughter and shout:

- *Dankon no ten mado!*
  The penis's heavenly window!

As the defiant gamblers played on, risking their lives with every throw of the dice, they updated the dashing image of the medieval *bakuto* gambler. If the men of old were swank, glamorous criminals who roamed the countryside, the new urban gamblers would be dashing but somewhat rougher and a good deal more streetwise. When asked their profession, they would answer *tengo* (trickster), *tego* ("prankster" in Mie dialect), or *tetengo* (hand trickster), all words for gamblers that are still used in today's underworld. Another popular gambling cognomen that has survived the centuries is *tekka uchi* (iron-fire bangers).

Tekka uchi appears as early as 1711 in a publication called *Konkō Kenshū*, which reports that it was used in the Shiga dialect in the south to mean "gambler," while *Hamogi–Sendai*, published in 1800, reports that *tekka uchi* was used in the Sendai region in the north to mean "rogue."

By the early twentieth century, the governments of the Meiji and Taisho periods had finally relaxed some of the more stringent anti-gambling laws; the West, after all, was more likely to be shocked by publicly impaled heads than by widespread betting. But by the beginning of the Showa period, with the rise of fascism, gambling once again became a perilous habit. Just as the cliques of the thirties were ready to surface, the government, in a spirit of wartime frugality, outlawed the manufacture of what it called *shashihin* (luxury products). Dice and flower cards were high on the list.

Today's betting scene developed from the turmoil of post-war Japan. The gambling cliques stuck together during the difficult war years, and after the war they expanded and opened their doors to thousands of new ethnic Korean and Chinese members. While the rest of Japan filled its speech with dapper American-sounding idioms, the outlawed gambling gangs followed the general underworld trend and sprinkled their language with Chinese and Korean words. By the late sixties, even the most orthodox Japanese gamblers had acquired exotic vocabularies that went well beyond mere gambling jargon. Shoes, for instance, were given Chinese slang names like *tā*, *chuira*, and *teito*. A male organ could be secretly referred to with the Chinese *toaten*, and a female organ with *kyari*. *Suicho* came to mean "dead as a doornail," *hairyan*, a "good-looking woman," and *ryanshan*, "torching a building." Words like *haraboji* and *chondai*, for "old man," came from Korean, as did *taru* (water), *tsuntsuroku* (bar), *shuni* (chicken), *chanpion* (money), *tarukichan* (housewife), and *nibutongi* (prostitute). By the seventies, gambling slang had become so exotic that even gamblers from different parts of town and with different gang affiliations had difficulty understanding each other's conversation.

- *Ano maotsu dare?* (Who's that cat's child?)
  Ee? (What?)
  Ano maotsu no mii! (That cat's child secret!)
  Ee? (What?)
  Ushi no tsume? (Cow's nails?)

Yā, uma no tsume! (No, horse nails!)

This might be decoded as:

Who's that foreign girl there?
What?
That foreign pro!
What?
D'you understand?
No, I don't understand.

Ushi no tsume (cow's nails) is standard underworld slang for "understand." The arcane reasoning behind the idiom is that a cow's nails are slit (*wakaru*), a verb that in Japanese also means to understand. A horse, on the other hand, does not have split nails, so *uma no tsume* (horse's nails) means "I do not understand."

Modern Parlors

The parlors the dice throwers frequent are in the shoddier parts of town, and are known as *semi* (the reversal of *mise*, "shop"). In the fifties and sixties, these gamblers invariably set up shop on the second floor of two-story shanties, a still-common practice. Should the police decide to raid the premises, an event known as *kari o kū* (eating the goose), the gamblers have time to throw their dice out of the window and quickly open a book.

Today many dice-throwing groups organize small illegal clubs in the backrooms of apartments, in a move known as *ichibahajime* (starting a market). These outfits are run along the same lines as the big Yakuza parlors, known as *jōbon* (permanent platters). These big outfits are stable and well-connected enough not to have to move around. A run-of-the-mill parlor is called *ginbari* (silver stretch), while a bustling concern that rakes in the cash is *kinbari* (golden stretch). These names, gangsters explain, were spawned by the word *yumihari* (stretched bow), an older term for betting parlor. The boss is *dōmoto* (stomach base), and his assistant *sukedekata* (helping-hand person). The *dekata* (hand person) collects the money and occasionally does *gomidashi* (throwing out the garbage), an unkind gambling term for showing unruly players the door. Larger backroom places also have a *chūban* (middle number), who brings tea or sake and helps clean up, a *tsubofuri* (dice shaker), and a *chūbon* (middle tray), who patrols the game.

- *Konna ni katchimatte, kono tsubofuri wa ore ni totteoki da ze!*
  I just keep on winning; that dice thrower's my favorite!
- *Ore wa anmari fukairi shitakunē kara, chūbon de jūbun sa.*
  I don't get too involved, you know, I just do the odd jobs here.

A lousy referee who has a history of letting games go awry is called *bonan* (dark tray).

- *Ano bonan ama da na! Kinō mo kizagoro ga koko de okottan da ze!*
  That manager's a real half ass! Yesterday there was another blowup!

(*Ama* is short for *amachua*, "amateur," and *kizagoro* refers to fighting with bits of broken glass.)

An illegal parlor worth its mettle has its stable of watchmen, who are known as *uyu* or *uwa*. The *denchū* (electric pole) and *bandachi* (standing watch) hang out on the street corner; *sotoban* (outside watch) guards the front door, and *hashigoban* (stair watch) guards the stairs. In the old-fashioned two-floor clubs, the senior watchman outside the parlor door is *nikaiban* (second-floor watch). If there is a raid, he and the *hashigoban* (stair watch) divert the officers long enough to let the gamblers make a getaway.

In the 1990s, the Japanese government launched a series of massive anti-mob campaigns that have forced the large Yakuza clans to curb some of their activities and step back into the shadows. There has subsequently been a trend called *naikai* (inside openings), with secret clubs being launched on a clan's territory without permission from the local boss and without the customary payola. The new-age gambling chieftain opens a whole line of these shops, leaving the work to assistants and partners. He is the *kasuri* (percentage maker), who commutes between parlors, collecting his percentages. These new places are called *shiki* (from *yashiki*, "premises"), and they operate in a way that dodges both the law and the underworld. This is called *shiromukku tekka* (banging in a white bridal gown).

9 ▪ Japanese Monkspeak

AMONG THE slang, jargon, and criminal lingoes that flourish on Japanese street corners, the boisterous X-rated language of the Buddhist clergy is by far the liveliest and most risqué. When Buddhist priests chatter among themselves, uninitiated eavesdroppers are left completely in the dark. Cryptic religious allusions, tilted metaphors, naughty classical puns, and words lifted from ancient texts leave even the most gifted Japanese slangmasters baffled.

- "What? You saw our venerable Buddha at the transformed palace?"
  "Yes, what a tunnel! It was only noon and he was already stock-still in heaven! He was handing over his eyes to a hell goblin!"
  "What? In broad daylight? The fried beans have flowered!"

This might be decoded as:

- "What? You saw our elderly Brother at the massage parlor?"
  "Yes, what an idiot! It was only noon, and he was

already drunk out of his mind! He was handing over his cash to a masseuse!"

"What? In broad daylight? I don't believe it!

The Japanese man or woman in the street would be scandalized to learn that venerable and ancient sects like the eight hundred-year-old Nichiren would have such a highly developed private slang. The priests maintain that without their lingo modern communication would grind to a halt. Buddhist doctrine insists that priests renounce all worldly habits, eat simple rice dishes, meditate, fervently chant lengthy sutras, and in every way follow in the footsteps of the Buddha. Modern priests, however, are no longer always celibate; some even marry, eat meat, and occasionally enjoy a sinful drink or two. Elderly religious leaders disapprove of modern secular trends, and desperate priests who wish to discuss anything from a simple pork chop to a multiple orgasm are forced to resort to code.

The priestly jargon is the oldest form of slang spoken in Japan today. Some of its words have been bandied about in monasteries since the Nara period (710–794 A.D.), when Buddhism struck firm roots throughout Japan. In the early days, pious priests initiated this slang by inventing pious euphemisms so as not to taint the inner sanctum with jarring worldly words. Whipping came to be called *nazu* (caressing), tears *shiotaru* (dropping salt), money *moku* (eyes), testicles *ryōgyaku* (spiritual globes), and restrooms *kishisho* (place of truth). Death, the ancient priests felt, was a particularly inelegant subject for discussion in a temple. Some of the pre-medieval euphemisms are still used by priests today: *agaru* (to rise), *tonzetsu* (abrupt termination), and *tsuchi ni naru* (becoming earth). The dead were referred to obliquely as *naorimono* (healed individuals) and *geshibutsu* (those transposed to Buddhahood), and cemeteries became *tsuchimura* (villages of earth). Suicide was dubbed *hishi* (untimely death) and, for the embarrassing occasion when a priest took his own life, his sect brothers would skirt reality with a quick *jigefutsu*, or "he turned himself into a Buddha."

As the private jargon took root the priests became more playful. If a priest, for instance, experienced an unexpected erection, his brothers would squeal a taunting *kotsuen hokki*, "sudden enlightenment" (a zesty pun on *kotsuen bokki*, "sudden erection"). Diarrhea was jocosely referred to as *rosetsu* (leaking garbage). A hemorrhoid flareup was called *akuhitsu* (bad handwriting), since *ji ga warui* can mean both "my Chinese characters are bad" and "my hemorrhoids are bad." *Kūkū jakujaku* (empty-empty sad-sad) came to mean that the priest had spent all his money on worldly goods and was now flat broke (i.e., his wallet is totally empty and he is totally sad). The secret monastic word for kissing became *kuan* (mouth relaxation).

- *Yā, washi wa kirei na onna o mita dake de—kotsuen hokki!*
  You know, when I see a beautiful woman—sudden enlightenment!
- *Ya sore o taberu to, itsumo rosetsu o shichatte dame nan desu yo.*
  When I eat that stuff, I always get the runs.
- *Hā, mattaku! Kyō wa kono akuhitsu no sei de, suwarē ya shinai yo.*

Man! My handwriting is so bad today, I can barely sit down.

- *Kūkū jakujaku de tabemono mo roku ni nai.*
 I'm so broke I can't even pay for food.
- *Sore de kuan shitan da? Mattaku omē to yū yatsu!*
 Then you kissed her? Oh, man!

The priests rejoiced in their secret slang. Even if their lives were fettered by strict ancient rules, their speech could run wild. *Geten* (non-Buddhist scriptures) came to mean pornography. Sexually attractive young women were referred to as *nōsha* (quick-witted individuals), and sexually attractive young men as *nōden* ("quick-witted fields," with field being priest slang for layman or non-priest). As tradition dictated that followers of the Buddha shave their heads, the skittish inside word for "priest" or "one of us" became *nagakami* (long-haired). The equally bald nuns were referred to as *menagakami* (long-haired females). Delicate novices who dated older priests were known as *zennanshi* (nice young boys).

As the clerics became more daring their language grew wittier and more blasphemous. The Buddha's name, which the devout dared not even pronounce, was bounced about, creating a barrage of daring new words. If a priest was stark naked he was said to be *hotsuro byakubutsu* (praying to the white Buddha). A *zokubutsu* (worldly Buddha) is a priest who is sexually very active. Secret Buddhas, *hibutsu*, are female organs (secret because they lie hidden behind panties), and *nurebotoke* (wet Buddhas) are post-coital male organs. *Nenju* and *nenbutsu* (intense praying), in which priests chant the Buddha's name in fervent rhythm, became code words for self-stimulation.

Bakebotoke (transformed Buddha) is a priest who enjoys wearing women's clothes during off-duty hours.

- *Fusuma o aketa totan, kare wa hotsuro byakubutsu de tsutatete, honto ni odorokimashita yo!*
  When I slid open that partition door, there he was, praying to the white Buddha. Man was I surprised!
- *Ano zokubutsu wa tera ni iru yori mo, kanrakugai ni iru jikan no hō ga nagai'n ja nai ka ne.*
  That worldly Buddha spends more time in the red-light district than he does in the temple.
- *Heya de nenju shiteru tokoro o mitsuketan desu yo.*
  I caught him praying intensely in his room.
- *Kinō nenbutsu no shisugi de asoko ga itakute!*
  I did so much intense praying yesterday, my thing aches!

Throughout the centuries, one of the toughest challenges facing the priests was the strict clerical ban on all meat, fish, and dairy products. A discreet nibble at a veal cutlet, a quick sip of milk, a tiny morsel of marinated raw fish, and future Buddhahood was in doubt. To avoid disclosing the sinful contents of a meal, faltering priests turned to their slang. One ancient trick was to bestow vegetarian names on even the heartiest meat dishes. Chickens, for instance, came to be known in the monasteries as *sanrisai* (vegetables that scramble over fences). Red meat was labeled *take* (mushroom). *Mōshari* (wad of rice) transformed itself into a pork chop, and *momiji* (maple leaves) became thin, succulent slices of fresh beef. Eel, one of the most prized delicacies, was given the code name *yama no imo* (mountain potato), and eggs were called *shironasu* (white eggplants).

Seafood has been traditionally granted loftier religious names. Fish, for instance, is sacrilegiously referred to as *butsu* (Buddha).

- *Kono butsu o nagameteru to, ogamitaku narimasu na!*
  Seeing the Buddha like this makes me want to kneel in prayer!
- *Yāa! Kono butsu no kaori wa mattaku subarashii desu yo ne!*
  Ooh, this smell of Buddha is driving me nuts!

Sashimi, raw slices of marinated fish, are known as *tanbutsu* ("gasping Buddha," as in gasping at the sheer deliciousness of the dish). Another irresistible delicacy, the octopus, was named after the Buddhist goddess of mercy *senju kannon* (Kannon of the Thousand Arms).

- *Dōka, dōka, hitokire de ii desu kara, sono kanbutsu itadakenai mono deshō ka?*
  Please, please, could I just have a teeny piece of gasping Buddha?
- *Mō nandemo ii kara! Senju kannon ogamashite kure!*
  I don't give a damn anymore! I'm going to pray to Kannon of the Thousand Arms!

Another fish that could cost a cleric his Buddhahood is the sumptuous sweetfish, which appears ominously in the priestly slang as *kamisori* (razor blade). Even more ominous is the sea bream. Priests refer to it as *shuza* (execution block).

- *Yoku minna no miteru mae de kamisori o nometa mon da!*

Right in front of everyone, he just swallowed that razorblade!
- *Shuza o itadakemasu ka na. Hara ga herimashita na.*
  Pass the execution block. I'm starving.

The stricter the monastery, the more inspired the words for food became. As the slang's vocabulary snowballed throughout the Middle Ages, even the meatless dishes served in monastic dining rooms were given cloak-and-dagger names. Some priests called tofu *shiratori* (white bird), others *terasakana* (temple fish). In temple-school slang the boring but wholesome devil's root paste that is served up day after day after day became known as *amidakyō* (Buddha's sutra, i.e. very long and very repetitive), and scallions are called *kannushi* (Shinto priests). Even the Buddha's bones (*shari*) were not spared; up to the late Edo period *shari* was an exclusively clerical word for rice. As the priests became more emancipated, affably socializing with the gangsters and criminals who hung out in downtown restaurants, *shari*, along with many other very private Buddhist words, hit the streets and was absorbed into the Yakuza mob's language.

Women and Wine

As priests fervidly swallowed "horse shoes" (*kanagutsu*—horse steaks), "dancing girls" (*odoriko*—eel), or snatched with their chopsticks at "rolled paper" (*makigami*—dry mackerel-shavings), many capped their sins with large swigs of *ten* (heaven) or alcohol. Nakamura Rengyo, in his *Bukkyō Dōgo Jiten* (Lexicon of Buddhist Language) blames a stanza in the eighth century *Nihon Shoki* (Chronicle of Japan) for sparking in ancient schoolboys the naughty equation of heaven and alcohol.

- *Konohanasakuya-hime ga Sanada no ine de ten no tamusake o kamoshita.*
  Princess Konohanasakuya with rice from Sanada created heaven-licking (extremely tasty) sake.

When a priest is said to be *tenchū* (a heaven addict) or *tenmei* (living for heaven), he is an alcoholic with little or no chance of ever reaching nirvana, the state of perfect blessedness. The only possible salvation would be what clerical slang calls *futen* (anti-heaven), giving up alcohol altogether. Priests, however, who enjoy their liquor have developed their own string of heavenly words. *Tenya*, (heavenly shop) is a bar or liquor store; *raten* (silk heaven) and *reiten* (cold heaven) both mean "chilled drink." If a wine has an exquisite bouquet, the word is *nōten* (adept heaven), while if it is no more than a foul grog the verdict is *hiuten* (negative heaven). If a priest runs out of alcohol, especially at night, and, desperately stalking the streets, finally manages to replenish his supply, the heavenly elixir obtained at such great personal risk is called *onten* (blessed heaven). *Fudōten* (stock still in heaven), means "completely inebriated."

- *Anta wa kono hiuten de washi o korosu ki ka ne?*
  Are you trying to kill me with this foul grog?
- *Oi! Chotto, chotto! Konna tokoro de onten nanka motette daijōbu kai?*

Hey! Wait a sec, wait a sec! D'you think it's OK to bring the blessed heaven in here?

- *Mappiruma kara fudōten ni naru nante omae-san ni wa akireta yo.*
  I just can't believe it's only noon and you're already totally stock still in heaven.

As this slang was flooded with "heavens" of every shape and caliber, circumspect monks invented a more esoteric set of alcoholic expressions. Discussing tea was one easy solution. *Ocha o itadakimasu ka na*, "I think I'll have some tea now," accompanied by a nudge, served as a clear signal to priests in the know. *Kōcha* (black tea), *bancha* (green tea), *mugicha* (barley tea), and *kobucha* (seaweed tea), are all expedient decoys. *Gyokuro*, a high-grade green tea made of an expensive blend of leaves, signals that the liquor under discussion is of the highest quality.

- *Moshi anta ga ato itteki demo kocha kuchi ni shitara, oshō san ni iitsukemasu yo!*
  If you take one more sip of that black tea, I'm telling the head priest!
- *Aā, mō tamaran'! Bancha ga dōshite mo hitsuyō ja!*
  I can't bear it any more! I need some green tea!
- *Kono mugicha chotto nonde goran! Aji wa ikaga ka na?*
  Take a swig of this barley tea! How's it taste?
- *Washi no heya ni kinasai—gyokuro o furumatte ageyō.*
  Come to my room—I'll treat you to some top-notch tea.

The early priests categorized the monastic pitfalls into three grades, and titled them *sanyoku no ō* (the three kingly desires). The first temptation was *jikiniku* (meat gobbling), the desire for tasty meat dishes. A close second was the craving for alcoholic beverages. The third and most dangerous of the kingly desires is *sokushin jōbutsu* (bringing one's body to Buddhahood), the secret monastic term for orgasm.

When a worldly priest cannot escape for a ribald night on the town, he might opt for what clerical slang calls *shumazuchō*, "a manual head-rub" (penile head, that is), also known as *shumagōzu*, "a pleasant manual head-rub."

- *Omae naka de shumazuchō shiten darō? Toire ni ikitain dakara hayaku dete kure yo!*
  What are you doing in there, a manual head-rub? Hurry up and come out, I need to use the toilet!
- *Saikin kare wa kao iro warui kedo, shumagōzu no shisugi no sei ja nai ka na.*
  He's been kinda pale lately. My guess is he's been doing too much pleasant manual head-rubbing.

Aroused priests trapped by the strict Buddhist demand for celibacy flooded their slang with chaste religious expressions that could double as covert references to self-stimulation. *Jiraku*, "self pleasure," is an abbreviation of *jijuhōraku*, "relishing the pleasure which accompanies the realization of the eternal truth." *Kaku sanmai ni iru* means "entering the state of enlightenment" (meditating by centering all one's thoughts on one object), and *jōrakugajo* means "eternal bliss."

- *Kiku tokoro ni yoru to, kare wa ichinichi ni nikai mo kaku sanmai ni iru.*

From what I hear, he enters the state of enlightenment at least twice a day.

- *Jōrakugajo ni wa ki o tsuketa hō ga ii yo.*
  Careful of that eternal bliss.

Other popular words for clerical self love are *yuiga dokuson* (the feeling of supremacy) and *daietsu*, which modern priests translate to mean "major pleasure." But Miguchi Sakae in *Ingo Kōsei no Yōshiki* (The Structure and Methodology of Clandestine Language) points out that its etymology is much more inspired. According to him, the witty priest who invented *daietsu* noticed that breaking the character *dai* (major) in two left the characters "single" and "person." (That same priest came up with *tenetsu* "heavenly pleasure," for sex. Undo the character *ten*, and you end up with "two" and "persons").

The largest body of priest-slang words for masturbation have to do with study and prayer. The playful notion is that a priest has two methods for reaching divine ecstasy: one is by focusing himself intensely on incanting verses from a sutra or the name of the Buddha, the other is by focusing himself intensely on his organ. In Nichiren circles this illicit shortcut is known as *ryakuhokeikyō* (abbreviated Lotus Sutra), *jirikishugyō* ("practicing asceticism with one's own power," as opposed to the power of the Buddha), or *jiriki ekō* (chanting sutras with one's own power).

- *Ichinichi sankai ryakuhokeikyō suru to wa, chotto yarisugi ja nai desu ka ne.*
  Doing the abbreviated Lotus Sutra three times in one day is a bit much, don't you think?

- *Ken no yatsu wa heya de jirikishugyō o surun ja nai ka.*
  I bet you Ken is in his room practicing asceticism using his own power.
- *Yā! Mezurashii! Jiriki ekō no shita koto ga nain desu ka?*
  What? You're kidding? You've never chanted sutras with your own power?

Other studious expressions for self-stimulation popular with the priests are *otenarai* (study), *shoshagyō* ("copying out a sutra by hand," a long and arduous task), and *dokuyugyō* (solitary pilgrimage). The scholarly joke behind the solitary pilgrimage is that the characters for *dokuyugyō* can also be read "to go and play by oneself."

When priests stimulate themselves in toilets, their good-natured brethren poke fun at them with *benjō shōganku* (perfect enlightenment in the restroom), or *benjō keraku* (divine pleasure and happiness in the restroom).

As a rule, Buddhist priests try to avoid dealing with their organs; some have even been known to commit *rasetsu* (penile chop), in which fanatic zealots, in an attempt to escape the passions of the flesh, sign up for surgery. The stricter the sect, the wilder the penile words grew. Excited priests invented drinking games that shocked even the most progressive criminal gangs in the pre-World War II bars. In the game *jushoku kanchō* (the responsible post of chief monk), a tipsy priest would leap up, unleash his organ, and bounce it onto his startled neighbor's head.

The bar rocked with laughter.

As the game caught on, it appeared around town as just *kanchō* (head priest), and soon more complicated variations like *machō* (penile top), became the craze.

The trick behind this game was not to just quickly wallop a head, but to rub one's organ back and forth over the victim's scalp for as long as possible. The bar parties grew wilder, and priests sat in rows playing *shuju chingan kii shimotsu* (penile assortment characteristics), with organs exposed, manipulated, and compared.

Back in the more innocent novice dormitories, romping teenagers played a similar game, cryptically named *rippei mashitsu* (standing-stick penile-knee). For accuracy during measuring, novices would kneel knee to knee, with the largest "standing stick" graduating into the inter-dormitory playoffs.

As priests struggled with celibacy their slang became more and more charged with words for penis. If they were not allowed to wield their organs, they could at least discuss them. By the mid-twentieth century, *mara* (devil), the most popular clerical slang term for penis, had spread from the monasteries through restaurants and bars into all areas of the underworld. The priests started using *rama* (the inversion of *mara*), but soon even respectable matrons were in the know, and old clerical favorites had to be resuscitated: *inmotsu* (hidden thing), *yōmotsu* (male thing), *haratake* (champignon), *shumoku* (bell hammer), and *bokken* (wooden sword).

- *Karera wa dōsei rama no koto shika atama ni wa nai deshō!*
  All those guys think about is devil.
- *Kare no koto dakara, furō de haratake demo aratterun deshō.*
  He must be in the bath washing his champignon as usual.

- *Hayaku sono shumoku o shimatte! Oshō ga kuru zo!*
  Quick, put your bell hammer away! The chief priest is coming!
- *Aitsu no bokken mita kai? Anmari ni dekakute tamagete shimaimashita yo!*
  Did you see his wooden sword? I couldn't believe how humongous it is!

Once more the Buddha became a major source of linguistic inspiration. An erect penis, for instance, was tagged as a *ritsuzō*, a statue of the standing Buddha. *Nikkei*, an even more scandalous metaphor, refers to the holy protuberance on the Buddha's brow (one of his thirty-two physical attributes). *Nikkei* took a twist when novices began using it for "breast." Semantic confusion ensued, and as the next generation of priests took office the new word *shimonikkei* (lower holy protuberance) was coined in an attempt to keep chests and penises apart.

During the penile games that novices and priests played, different types of organs were given different names. Stiffness and sexual endurance were important in a winner, and *kongo rama* (from *kongo mara*, "indestructible penis") was the best organ contestants could hope for. Runners-up are *nōgu*, "agile tool," *renkon*, "disciplined root," *kiishimotsu*, "eccentric and strange thing" (not much to look at but quite potent), and *chikuhei*, "teakwood stick," for tough if not large organs. A penis with a slim shaft but large top is *zuidai konshō*, "head-large root-small." On the other side of the scale are *kunpei*, "smelly sticks," and, at the bottom of the barrel, *zōroku*, "turtle-six." (Not only is this penis hairless like a turtle, but its "shell" or foreskin is so tight that, pull as one may, the head does not come out.)

- *Kare wa zōroku to kikimasu kara, mattaku yaku ni tatan' deshō.*
  They say his dick's turtle-six—poor guy.
- *Kare no kongo rama wa mattaku rippa desu ne!*
  Man, his indestructible penis is real ace!
- *Watashi wa jibun no renkon ni wa jishin ga arun desu yo.*
  I know I can rely on my disciplined root.

If a man is young and virile his organ is labeled *mugai* (uncovered), the argument being that penises in their prime spend more time out of than in their owners' apparel. An elderly organ, on the other hand, is called *dongon reki* (slow-root feeble-machine).

At the bars and restaurants priests met women from all walks of life. The *gōsha* (powerful individuals), women with bulging muscles and an uncanny ability to hold their liquor; *chimisha* (individuals who know the taste), active virgins who specialize in fellatio and anal sex; *kōsha* (individuals who like it), women who enjoy one-night stands with priests; *ansha* (dull individuals), women who are easily tricked; and *nōsha* (able individuals), women of exceptional beauty. In wilder taverns they met "female saints" (*onna hijiri*), gruff women who like disguising themselves as men; "changed roots" (*tenkon*), women who had been men until they had had an operation; "double root" (*nikon*), elegant hermaphrodites; "double-shaped individuals" (*nigyōsha*), men with breasts; and "plover birds" (*chidori*), men in women's clothes.

The priests also met professional women. *Kabosatsu* (singing bodhisattvas) were the accomplished geisha who could freshen up any party with sprightly conversation and masterly tunes. They might also encounter *tsujisha*, "street corner individuals," and *mameuri*, "bean sellers" ("bean" as in sexual organ), women who, selling sexual favors, are a guaranteed ticket to hell for a Buddha-fearing priest. Dangerous women working in red-light massage parlors and soapland sex-bathhouses are given hellish titles such as *yashanyo*, a fearsome Sanskrit demon who eats men, *jigokuki* (hell goblin), and *gokusha* (individual from hell).

- *Asoko ni namamekashii mameuri ga tatte orimasu zo!*
  Look at those slick bean sellers standing there!
- *Shintaro no tsure no onna wa, jitsu o yū to gokusha nan desu yo.*
  That woman with Shintaro, she's an individual from hell.
- *Koko wa jigokuki bakkari de kanawan'.*
  I can't stand it here, it's teeming with hell goblins.

Priests ranked intercourse with a prostitute among the most dangerous of sins, and branded it as *dagoku* (falling to hell). One way to soften the evil was to practice *hishi* (no center), where a cleric paid a woman to manipulate him from head to toe, carefully steering clear of his "center." Priests, however, who yielded to professional intercourse, were accused of passionate entanglement (*kyōraku*), waving their wooden swords (*bokken o furu*), mixing lewdly (*kojin*), and even banging (*utsu*).

Thesaurus

THIS THESAURUS is a representative selection of Japanese slang terms arranged alphabetically under English subject headings. It is designed to give the reader both an overview of some of the words featured in this book, and to introduce topics of a wider scope, such as terms for money, prison, drugs, and alcohol.

Most of the expressions are *ingo* (hidden language)—the pithiest slang and jargon spoken in underworld cliques throughout Japan. As these *ingo* words have a tendency to remain firmly encapsulated in the speech of particular groups, urban or regional, foreigners who try them out on the wrong crowd will be met with at best blank stares, at worst with shock and terror.

ALCOHOL

atapin bad sake (from *atama*, "head" and *pin*, "boing")

awa foam beer

awagisu foam liquor

kiyoiwake (from *kiyoi*, "clear," and *wake*, Ainu word for "water")

nigagisu bitter liquor

teppen scalp (bad sake)

ANAL INTERCOURSE

bakonbakon suru doing bang bang

dandan fuku gradual wipe

dandan suru doing it gradually

rishi o giru ripping the ass (inversion of *shiri o giru*)

uraguchi nyūgaku entering school through the back door (college slang)

uramontsuko going through the back gate

ANUS

akabe (western Japanese dialect origin)

ana hole

gebo

gesu also means "bottom"

gesu no ana

gobō no kirikuchi cut burdock

ikihiri

ikimi breathing body (northern Japanese dialect origin)

ishiki (Hiroshima slang)

isuke (southern Japanese dialect origin)

keppo (Hiroshima dialect)

kukka

kusube

okama iron pot (more popular as a word for "homosexual")

shigame anus (northern Japanese dialect origin)

unpan (central Japanese dialect origin)

uramon back door

ARREST, to

bakuru

hikkakeru to hook

kanakakeru to put metal on

kuikomu to gnaw into (as a dog does)

mushi

nejiru to wrench

nekaru

neru to sleep

nezumaki citizen's arrest

shimeru to throttle

ARRESTED, to be

anberu to be punched (Nagasaki slang)

bare (Kyushu dialect origin)

barareru from *hippararereu*

chaburu

daimaki ni au to meet on the platform (to be

arrested at the scene of
the crime)
datsumaki ni au
donten (northern Japanese
dialect origin)
dōroku nekari to be arrested
at the scene of the crime
furi disadvantage
hipparareru
jime ni kakaru to be tied up
kakaru to be tied up
kamaru from *tsukamaru*, "to
catch"
kanakakeru to put on metal
karidasu to take out
kokeru to fall
kuzureru to collapse
machiba ni kakaru to be
caught at the waiting
place (to be arrested in a
police net)
moka
nashi o utsu

nukaru to bungle
shibakareru to be arrested
on the job
son o suru to get lost
sukatenpura subordinate
offering himself up for
arrest in place of his
boss (from *suka*,
shortened inversion of
kawasu, "exchange," and
tenpura)
tana o utsu to hit the shelf
tananashi nibaru
tenpura Japanese deep-
fried food (from the
image that the arrested
criminal feels like he is
about to be dropped into
a cauldron of boiling fat)
teire crackdown
teyao chora (ethnic Chinese
origin)
tsuru to fish

ARSON

aka ga iku the red goes
aka hashiru the red runs
aka neburu the red licks
aka ga iku the red goes
akainki red ink
akainu red dog
akainu o awaseru to make
the red dogs meet
akamaru red circle ("fire" in
Nagasaki slang)
akamushi red insect
akamushi hau the red insect
crawls

akaneko red cat
akaneko barasu to kill the
red cat
akaneko o owasu to flay the
red cat
akaneko o hawasu to make
the red cat crawl
akauma red horse
akauma o keshikakeru to get
the red horse going
akauma tobasu to make the
red horse fly
akaume red plum

ARSON *(continued)*

atatameru to warm up

beni o tsukeru to put on
lipstick

chitsurarā (ethnic Korean
origin)

hairyanzu (ethnic Chinese
origin)

kobiyaotta (ethnic Korean
origin)

ryanshan suru (ethnic
Chinese origin)

teka o keru to kick the
brightness

tera o kakeru to illuminate

terashi o kameru

ARSONIST

aite individual who steals
from a burning house
(police slang)

akainu red dog

akaneko red cat

akauma red horse

chiyotandā (ethnic Korean
origin)

sōtarucha (ethnic Korean
origin)

sōtaura (ethnic Korean
origin)

BREASTS

chichi (general slang)

oppai (general slang)

nonchichi contraction of
none and *chichi*, "breast"

paiotsu inversion of *oppai*

(criminal slang)

pechapai contraction of
pecha, "flattened," and
oppai, "breast"

rēzunpai raisin pie

BUTTOCKS

akabe also means "anus"

danbe large, prominent
bottom (southwestern
Japanese dialect origin)

denbo from *denbu*, "bottom"

denbu bottom (standard
word)

deko (Ishikawa dialect)

gesu also means "anus"

hechibetta buttocks
(western Japanese
origin)

heppe (northern Japanese
dialect origin)

hichipeta buttocks (western
Japanese origin)

hitabira (Kagoshima slang)

hitsube

jigo (Nagasaki slang)

ketsu ass (standard word)

ketsumedo (Osaka slang)

kechi dialect version of *ketsu*, "ass"

kechipeta (northeastern Japanese dialect origin)

kikuza chrysanthemum

kikurage edible tree fungus

mappo end tail

momojiri peach bottom (fat, prominent bottom)

rishi inversion of *shiri*, "bottom"

shinbita

shippe from *shippo*, "tail"

shippeta

shippo tail

shikko (southwestern Japanese dialect origin)

shiri (standard slang)

shiribachi ass pot

shiropo (central Japanese dialect origin)

shitakuchi lower mouth (homosexual jargon)

subo (Wakayama dialect origin)

sunnoko (central Japanese dialect origin)

supetta (northwestern Japanese dialect origin)

tanpo

tsube (Shikoku island dialect)

usu woman's bottom

zugo (southern Kyushu island slang)

CAR

guru short for *kuruma*, "car"

hayaguru from *haya*, "fast" and *kuruma*, "car"

oto short for *otomachiku*, "automatic"

makuru inversion of *kuruma*, "car"

rukuma inversion of *kuruma*, "car"

CIGARETTE

ahōgusa fool's weed

bakota inversion of *tabako*, "cigarette"

bata short for *batako*, an inversion of *tabako*, "cigarette"

batako inversion of *tabako*, "cigarette"

danyaku ammunition

enko

entotsu

jikitabako immediate cigarette (cigarette smoked after a meal)

kasumi haze

katome

kemu short for *kemuri*, "fumes"

CIGARETTE (continued)

kemuri fumes
kenzaki (northern Japanese dialect origin)
kisuri (northern Japanese dialect origin)
kumo cloud
makimoya rolled haze
moku piece
mokumo version of *moku*
moya haze

neta seed
okā-san mommy
rōzu waste
ta short for *tabako*, "cigarette"
tāko short for *tabako*, "cigarette"
uma horse
yani tar
zome

CONDOM

furenchi retā French letter
gomu rubber
gorōbu globe
kondo-san Mr. Condo(m)
naito kyappu nightcap
nuigurumi stuffed toy
reinkōto raincoat

reinkyappu rain cap
rūde-sama Lord Ruede, from the German *Ruedesack*
sayagoromo night attire
sukin skin

CONDOM, break

kinugoshi silk through which bean curd is

usually strained
pinhoru pin hole

CONDOMLESS

junnama pure raw
nama raw

sumara pure penis

DIARRHEA

agahara from *akahara*, "red belly"
hara o sageru dropping the belly
haratosu stomach rush
harahashiri belly run

harakudari belly decent
harakudashi belly purge
harasage belly drop
kudarikuso descending shit
pippi (onomatopoeic)

DRUGS

bākubure morphine (Korean origin)

butsu thing

eru the initial L, short for LSD

funmatsu flour (heroin and other white powder drugs)

hashishi hashish

koka coca (short for cocaine)

kusuri medicine

matsu powder (heroin, white powder drugs)

merikenko American seed (drugs imported to Japan from the USA)

shabu from *shaburu*, "suck up"

shiro white (heroin and other white powder drugs)

sukuri from *kusuri* (medicine or drugs in general)

yakuneta poisonous seed (bad quality drugs)

yuki snow (heroin or cocaine)

DRUGS, amphetamines

hiropon from its medical name "philopon"

pon short for *hiropon*

DRUGS, heroin

eichi the initial H, short for "heroin"

hero short for "heroin"

kona flour (heroin)

nako inversion of *kona*, "flour" (heroin)

neta inversion of *tane*, "seed" (heroin)

mabuneta shining seed (good quality heroin)

nanbā yon number four (high quality heroin from Hong Kong)

pe from *he*, the first syllable of "heroin" (as *he* means "fart" in Japanese, drug cliques changed *he* to *pe*)

rohe inversion of hero, "heroin"

tane seed (heroin)

DRUGS, marijuana

choko (high school slang)

happa leaves

kusa grass

marifana Japanese pronunciation of "marijuana"

DRUGS, opium

ahen opium (standard Japanese)
chiyakusatsui to smoke opium (Korean origin)
kuro black
nama raw
togi (Korean origin, Hoenyong dialect)
tsugaru opium grown in Tsugaru in northern Japan
yāpin from the Chinese word *yāpyan*

DRUGS, paint thinner

anpan bean-jam bun
fūsen balloon
shina the English word "thinner"

DRUGS, pills

batankyū wham bang (take a pill and your head hits the pillow)
hai-chan little Mr. High
iipin prescription pills
megumi no piru happy pills
okei-chan little Mr. OK (drug in pill form)

EJACULATE, to

buppanasu to totally let go
deru to come out
dasu to send
iku to go
naku to cry, to howl
nukani to ejaculate twice in a row (contraction of *nukanai*, "without taking out" and *ni*, "two")
rariru to flip out
uchidome ni suru to bring a show to a close

ERECTION

asadachi morning stand (morning erection)
bin bin boing boing
bokki erection (standard)
kōkachin from *kōka*, "stiff" and *chin*, "penis"
pin boing
tento o haru to put up a tent
uiri wheelie (high school slang)

ERECTION, loss of

chinbotsu sinking
fuyakeru to become sodden
naeru to wither

kesu to extinguish
ojigi suru to bow
shioreru to droop

ESCAPE

agaru to rise
akeru to become empty
bakoshi to escape the police
    by leaving town
barashi to knock off, to
    violate (escape from the
    police or from jail)
batarakō (pickpocket slang)
buruya suru inversion of
    yaburu, "to break" (to
    break out of jail)
chiimau
chōhō to drag out one's
    breath (ethnic Chinese
    slang)
doromu (criminal jargon)
doron disappear
esu the initial S, short for
    "escape"
fukeru
geso o haku to wear shoes
    (the image is that of
    putting one's shoes on
    and running)
geso o hayameru to acceler-
    ate the tentacles (*geso is
    street* slang for "legs")
gesozuru to rub the
    tentacles (*geso* is street
    slang for "legs" or

"shoes" and implies "to
    run fast")
gorokoshi o fukeru
hajiku to bounce up
hako o tsukau to use the box
    (to escape by train)
itachi suru to do weasel (to
    escape by dodging
    police lines)
kama o tsuku to bang the
    ass (to escape and then
    hide)
kazurahige to escape from
    the police (from *kazura*,
    an inversion of *zurakaru*,
    "to run for it," and *hige*,
    "whiskers," a slang
    word for police)
ketsubaru to stretch one's
    ass
kiirora (ethnic Korean
    origin)
miruichiya (ethnic Korean
    origin)
mochizura from *mochi*, "to
    hold," and *zurakaru*, "to
    escape" (to escape with
    the loot)
muguru to escape from the
    police or from jail

ESCAPE *(continued)*

nagashikumu from *nagashi-komu*, "to pour" (to leave town)

nobiru to extend (to leave town)

rāhowa to pick flowers (ethnic Chinese origin)

rakan from *zurakaru*, "to escape"

rakaru from *zurakaru*, "to escape"

sāya sāya (ethnic Korean origin)

shunshuryū to flow with the current (ethnic Chinese origin)

tachikorobi stand and roll (escape after one has been arrested by the police)

takatobi suru to fly high

teirōchirō (ethnic Chinese origin)

teitsutā (ethnic Korean origin)

tsura tsura to escape after a criminal job

tsugumu to hide from the police after a crime

yasa o kaeru to change house (to escape by leaving town)

EXCREMENT

enko

kōku Coke (high school slang idea taken from the Japanese Coca Cola ad campaign "I feel Coke," meaning "I feel refreshed")

kuso feces (standard word)

kyūjū nineteen (the alternative reading of *kuso*, "feces")

morimori thick wad

noguso field shit (excreting outdoors)

onkobo (dialect origin)

ōkii no big one (high school slang)

ōkii yatsu big guy (high school slang)

ōmusubi the big finish

ōzume grand finale

toguro coil (student slang)

unchi from the standard word *unko*, "feces"

unko feces (standard word)

FELLATIO

fera short for *ferachio*, "fellatio"

furūto flute

kokku sakkingu from the

English "cock sucking"
kyandē candy
ofera from the Japanese *fera*
  with an honorific "*o*"

ōraru sekkusu oral sex
shakuhachi flute

FELLATIO, with condom
ofera kabuse fellatio with
  cover

surippu slip (contraction of
  "skin lip")

FELLATIO, without condom
nama ensō raw perfor-
  mance
namafera raw fellatio (from
  nama, "raw" and *fera*,

  "fellatio")
namajaku from *nama*
  shakuhachi, "raw flute"
nama shakuhachi raw flute

FLATULENCE
būbū (onomatopoeic)
būsuka (onomatopoeic)
demono eruption
he (standard word)
nigirippe clasped fart
  (game where one farts
  into one's hand and

  holds it up to a friend's
  face)
onara sound
sukashipe transparent fart
  (discreet flatulence)
tsukambe catching the fart
  (synonym of *nigirippe*
  game)

GOODBYE
bainara fusion of "bye" and
  sayonara (high school
  slang)
baicha swanker version of
  the childish *haichai*,
  "toodle-loo" (high
  school slang)
barasa inversion of *saraba*,

  "farewell" (high school
  slang)
bayonara fusion of "bye"
  and *sayonara* (high
  school slang)
ibaiba inversion of "bye
  bye" (high school slang)

GUN

buchitani (ethnic Korean origin)

chori (ethnic Chinese origin, from *che zhi*, "bullet machine")

haji from *hajiki*, "spring"

hajiki spring, gun-cock

hatsu discharge

higa

ho (ethnic Korean origin)

hōtsu (ethnic Chinese origin)

hōshinhii (ethnic Chinese origin, from *hu shen pi*, "body-guarding piece")

hōteiyotsu (ethnic Chinese origin)

higa

kikai machine

mutsukai (ethnic Korean origin, Yongwan dialect)

nigiri clutch

nonbo

pachinko pinball machine

penra (Chinese origin, from *bian le*, "at one's side")

tāchiitsu (ethnic Chinese origin)

tai sleep (ethnic Korean origin)

tan from *tanjū*, "revolver"

tējitari pig's leg (ethnic Korean origin)

tobi short for *tobidōgu*, "flying tool"

tobidōgu flying tool

toyachitari pig's leg (ethnic Korean origin)

HANDCUFFS

chin

hanamae in front of the nose

kai shells

kakushi hidden (the police will often allow one to drape a jacket over one's handcuffs)

shaka Buddha

wappa rings

HOMOSEXUAL

anko (Yakuza slang)

botsu (Yakuza slang)

bonpu mortal (homosexual slang)

eichi bii the initials HB, short for "homo boy" (student slang)

emu-teki "M-like"; the initial M stands for "masculine" (butch-looking, straight-acting homosexual)

gei the English word "gay"

gei bōi gay boy (host in a homosexual club)

girimomu (Yakuza slang)

hādo gei hard gay (tough-looking homosexual)

hādo koa hardcore (tough-looking homosexual)

homo homo

ichi (Yakuza slang)

isha no musuko doctor's son (they get into university through the "back door")

kikuzara

musume daughter (prison slang)

neko cat (passive, effeminate homosexual)

nisai older man who prefers young men (homosexual slang)

ome

okama (general slang)

okamahori ass digger

onē sister

rishi inversion of *shiri*, "bottom"

tachiyaku actor playing a leading man (tough-acting, masculine homosexual)

tonko adolescent homosexual (Yakuza slang)

ukemi receiving body (passive, effeminate homosexual)

yakko servant (prison slang)

IDIOT

aho (Osaka dialect origin)

ahondara (Osaka dialect origin)

anpontan (Tochigi dialect origin)

ao from *aho*

atama ga piiman red-pepper head

atama ga supagetti spaghetti head

atama ga uni sea-urchin head

atatakai warm

ateuma whipped horse (gambling slang)

attamon from *atatakai mono*, "warm person"

āpā contraction of *atama*, "head" and *pā*, "soft-headed"

baka (standard slang)

bakachin (standard slang)

bakamono (standard slang)

bobura

boke idiot

boketan stronger version of *boke*

dabo from *dabohaze*, "goby fish"

daburu pā conjunction of the English word "double," and *pā*, "soft-headed"

dara from *daradara*, "slip-shod"

daraji

IDIOT *(continued)*

dongodara

donkō slow train (high school slang)

donkusai

donpo

ei eichi ō the letters AHO which spell *aho* (high school slang)

hekoki farter

hetare farter

ketsunuke assless

momi unhulled kernel of rice (gambling slang)

nōtarin from *nō*, "brain," and *tarinai*, "is lacking"

noppo tall and gangly (gambling slang)

noroma (dialect origin)

ō-chan contraction of "oxygen," and *chan*, "little Mr." (student slang)

onchi tone-deaf

otankonasu (Tochigi dialect origin)

pā soft-headed

pābo from *pā*, "idiot"

pākingu fusion of *pā*, "soft-headed," and "king" (high school slang)

pāpurin (high school slang)

pāpurishū (high school slang)

paparapa (onomatopoeic) version of *pā*, "soft headed"

ponke (dialect origin)

rējii short for *kurējii*, the English word "crazy"

shirinuke assless

taka (gambling slang)

tari short for *tarinai*, "lacking"

tawake romper (Nagoya dialect origin)

toroi dull

usunoro from *usui*, "weak," and *noroi*, "slow"

KILL, to

chirasu to scatter

higehachiya (ethnic Korean origin)

honaira (ethnic Korean origin)

honengu (ethnic Korean origin)

mageru to twist

nemurasu to put to sleep

nesaseru to put to sleep

nishi o mukasu to make someone face west (bodies buried according to Buddhist custom, have their heads pointing west)

shimeru to close

shinginta (ethnic Korean origin, "to make cold," Seoul dialect)

tatamu to fold
tomeru to stop

yaru to do

KNIFE

ai short for *aikuchi*
aikuchi dagger
aikusu from *aikuchi*
bade inversion of *deba*, short for *debabōchō*, "kitchen knife"
dosu from *odosu*, "to threaten"
haku knife that has been used in a robbery or stabbing
kōchō cooking knife (dialect origin)
koburi small thin-bladed knife

nagashari noodle
nareteru it becomes familiar (central Japanese dialect origin)
nonbo can also mean "gun"
nuki
saka small, sharp knife made in Osaka
tenshi
ya
yaiba
yappa
yasu lance

LOCK PICKING

ate o tsukau to use a chisel
atetsukai chiseling
eri o kiru to cut a collar, to destroy the lock
eri o tsukeru to put on a collar (pun on *iri o tsukeru*, "using to enter")
eri o tsuneru to nip a collar
eritsuke with collar
geri o tsukeru to use a jigger
hana o konasu to handle flowers
hana o toru to pick flowers
hanaseburu breaking the front part of the lock
iri o keru to kick the entry

iritsukeru using to enter
iso o tsukeru to use a jigger
koburu to widget (to break the lock)
konasu to grind (to open with a master key)
mushi o toru to take an insect
shiburu to widget (to break the lock)
shimeage screwing on
shimeru to strangle
tanka o hiraku to burst out swearing (to break a lock with force)
tanka tsuru to fish the door

LOCK PICKING (continued)

tate o kiru to cut that which stands

tehataki to get rid of by hand

LOCK PICKING, tools

ai short for *aikagi*, "master key"

aibiki trick

aikagi master key

aisu Osaka street slang

akinogassan Mount Akino

ate chisel

gen chord

geri jigger

harigane wire

hikkake hook

kenuki tweezers

kenukimusō matchless tweezers

koburi widget

kōchō cooking knife

kuwa hoe

makkeita master key (ethnic Korean origin)

neji wrench

nezumi mouse

pasu pass, as in "pass key"

sanpira master key

sanya master key

MASTURBATION

emu the initial M, short for *masutabēshon*, "masturbation"

henzuri Osaka dialect version of *senzuri*, "thousand rubs"

hitori de yaru doing it by oneself

hitorigokko self-play

jibun de jaru doing it on one's own

kawatsurumi skin copulation (male masturbation)

kawatsururi skin sliding (male masturbation)

masu "mas" (short for "masturbation")

masu kagami masturbation in front of a mirror; pun on Sei Shonagen's medieval literary work *Masukagami* (The Pillow Book)

senzuri thousand rubs (standard slang)

shikoshiko rub rub

suma no ura suma backwards (which spells *masu*, short for "masturbation")

sutabēshon "'sturbation"

zurisen inversion of *senzuri*, "thousand rubs"

MASTURBATION, female

ateire blocking and entering

bobowaru cunt splitting

botantori button grabbing (stimulating the clitoris)

ijirimakurimawasu to finger in, out, and around

ijirimakuru to finger round and round

ijirimawasu to finger all around

irau (Osaka slang origin)

irou (Osaka slang origin)

kaisenzuri shell thousand-rubs

manzuri ten thousand rubs

nigiribobo grab cunt

omankosuri cunt rub

omekosuri Osaka slang version of *omankosuri*

suichi o ireru flicking the switch (stimulating the clitoris)

temanko hand cunt

temeko hand cunt

ude ningyō hand doll

yubi ningyō finger doll

yubi zeme finger attack

MENSTRUATION

aka red

akamanman red cunt-cunt

akauma red horse

hatabi flag day (the Japanese flag being a red dot on a white background)

emu the initial M, short for "menstruation"

furawā from the English flower (college slang)

honchū during the red

jamupan jelly roll (high school slang)

kagome-chan little Miss Kagome (high school slang from "Kagome," the brand name of a ketchup)

kame from the English "came," as in "my period has come"

reddo zōnu red zone (college slang)

tenashi no hands (in the past women were not allowd to cook during menstruation)

MONEY

ago jaw (the money that a masseuse pays her parlor for food)

akanama red raw (small change)

arumono from *aru*, "to

MONEY *(continued)*

have," and *mono*, "thing"

ashi leg (cab fare that escort agencies charge clients when prostitutes do out-calls)

asuke

baiūnen 105 years (ethnic Chinese origin)

bira leaflet

chibuseki (ethnic Korean gambling slang)

chōsōi (ethnic Korean origin)

chōzenmuri (ethnic Korean origin)

dende (dialect origin)

egoro the name *Egoro* (traditional actor slang)

emu the initial M, short for "money"

gasehin counterfeit money

gasetsū counterfeit money

gennama hard cash

higo protection

hin goods

hinta

hitsuji sheep (paper money, as sheep eat paper)

huan huan joy joy (ethnic Chinese origin)

kami paper

kan (pickpocket slang)

kuruji (ethnic Korean origin)

kyasshu the English word "cash"

mamono the real thing

manē the English word "money"

mi

mii-manē one's own money (from the English words "me," and "money")

mii-gane one's own money (fusion of the English word "me," with *gane*, "money")

mizu water

moku eyes (priest slang)

nama raw

namagen inversion of *gennama*, "hard cash"

nema inversion of *manē*, the English "money"

nē mon from *nai mono*, "non-existing thing"

oashi the honorific prefix "*o*" and *ashi*, "leg"

ochizeni dropped cash (money lost at gambling) (gambling slang)

oshin "*o*" added to *shin* (Tokyo criminal slang for "money")

pēpā the English word "paper"

riki convenience

ru Chinese reading of the character *nagare*, "to flow"

seke (ethnic Korean origin, Cholla Namdo dialect)

shan (ethnic Chinese origin)

shin short for *shinta*

shinta Tokyo slang version of *hinta*

sokiyu (ethnic Korean origin)

tarechi paper money (ethnic Korean origin)

tarō the name *Tarō*

tsū short for *tsūka*, "currency"

tsūpin taken from *tsūka*, "currency," and *pin*, "money"

tsura face

ura back

watari handing over

zeni (standard word)

zenko (Hokkaido slang version of *zeni*)

zenzen none at all

zeze dialect version of *zeni*

zezeko (central Japanese dialect origin)

MONEY, counterfeit

anko bean jam (bundle of fake cash)

dosa from *dosha*, "soil"

dosha soil

gakusai

gasehin contraction of *gase*, "fake," and *hinta*, "money"

gaseneta fake seed

gasetan

gasetsū contraction of *gase*, "fake," and *tsūka*, "currency"

kakusai

neta inversion of *tane*, "seed"

nyūiri from *nyū*, "insert" and *iri*, "enter" (counterfeit bills that are inserted among real yen notes)

pā worthless

satsu bank note

tsukegi spill

yama mountain

PENIS

aporo Apollo (college slang)

are that

ashi leg

asoko over there

atama head (glans of the penis)

bidenbō (Yakuza slang)

bō rod

bōdō (Yakuza slang)

bōringu driller

bōsan priest

burakujakku black jack (college slang)

chāji battery charge (college slang)

chako (western Japanese dialect origin)

PENIS (continued)

chanbe (central Japanese dialect origin)

chimaki rice dumpling wrapped in bamboo leaves

chinboko (northern Japanese dialect origin)

chinchin (standard slang)

chinpo (standard slang)

chinpoko (standard slang)

chinko (standard slang)

chintama from *chin*, "penis," and *tama*, "balls"

chipō dialect version of *chinpo*

dama from *tama*, "testicles," also used to mean "penis"

danbira broad sword (Yakuza slang)

dankon male root (standard expression)

danbe (northern Japanese dialect origin)

danbo (Hiroshima slang)

danpe (northern Japanese dialect origin)

dappe (dialect origin)

debi (Yakuza slang)

debibo (Yakuza slang)

dechibō from *detchibō*

deibo

dekademo

demo

deresuke philanderer

deretsuku to dally, to dangle

deshi adherent, pupil

detchi apprentice

detchibō apprentice stick

dōgu tool

emu the initial M, short for the penile synonym *musuko*, "son"

etchimotsu dialect version of *ichimotsu*, "one thing"

ete strong point

etekichi from *ete*, "strong point" and the name-ending *kichi*

farosu phallus (college slang)

fuigo forge

fukubebā

fukubepā (Yakuza slang, related to *fukube*, "vagina")

furumaru (northern Japanese dialect origin)

gaijin outside person, foreigner

gamo from *kamo*, "duck"

gamoko from *gamo*, "duck," and *ko*, "child"

gan wild goose

gankubi pipe head

ganshu neck of a wild goose (penile shaft)

gari (central Japanese dialect version of *kari*, "goose")

genyō (Yakuza slang)

genki lively, healthy

genzō (Yakuza slang)

goyō no mono useful thing

gobō burdock

gyokukei jewel stem

hanamoto nose root

hashira pole

henoko (central Japanese dialect origin)

heppe (northern Japanese dialect origin)

hidenbō secret stick

hode (Yakuza slang)

hōshin gun barrel

hōtōbōzu debauched little boy

ichimatsu from *ichimotsu*, "one thing"

ichimotsu article, thing

ikebachi living pot

ikita animate

imo potato

imoko from *imo*, "potato," and *ko*, "child"

ingakotsu karma bone

inkei hidden stem

isejishi (archaic)

itsubutsu excellent specimen

jiji (northeastern Japanese dialect origin)

jijiko from *jiji*

jijinbō (Niigata dialect origin)

kame turtle

kamo duck

kare he, him

kari wild goose

karikubi goose neck (shaft of the penis)

ke hair

keppe (northern Japanese dialect origin)

ketō hairy foreigner (popular slang in the 40s and 50s)

kihai (criminal jargon)

kiri drill

kitō cylinder

kokku cock (student slang)

kozō small child

kurobē proper name

kyūri cucumber

maeashi front leg

maemon front thing

mara (standard slang)

marage from *mara*, "penis," and *ge*, "hair"

matsutake mushroom

miminashiunagi earless eel

moderugan model gun (student slang)

mono thing

musuko son

nabusa dialect word for "snake"

naga ashi long leg (northern Japanese dialect slang)

naka ashi inside leg

nakaore middle crease

nankon male root

nankotsu soft bone

ne root

nikubachi meat pot

nikubashira meat pole

nikubō meat stick

nobichijimi expansion and contraction

noko short for *takenoko*, "bamboo"

PENIS *(continued)*

nukimi drawn sword (also means "naked man")

nyōdō urine way

obashira male pole

odogu male tool

ohashi male edge

ohasse from *ohashi*, "male edge"

ohozo male navel

oninnin (general slang euphemism)

otoko no shinburu man's symbol

otoko no shōchō man's emblem

otokone man's root

pisuton piston (college slang)

pochi inversion of *chinpo*

pochin inversion of *chinpo*

pokochin inversion of *chinpoko*

rakkyō scallion

reji

reki

reko inversion of *kore*, "this"

reji

rosen oar peg

roten from *rosen*

sabe (from the proper name Sakubei)

sade

sakasaboko upside-down sword

sakubei (proper name)

sakuzō (proper name)

san son

sao pole

segare son

shinji (northeastern Japanese dialect origin)

shinjiko from *shinji*

shiromono article, thing

sōbakui (ethnic Korean origin)

suboke naked craze

sukuryū screw (college slang)

surikoki pestle

suyari naked spear

suzu bell

takenoko bamboo

tama ball (usually used to mean testicles)

tanbe (western Japanese dialect origin)

teko lever

teibo

tengu long-nosed goblin

teppō gun

tere (southwestern Japanese origin)

terekuso (Shikoku island version of *tere*)

tokobashira bed stick

totchin (Kyushu island dialect origin)

tsuno horn

tsuchi sledgehammer

tsuka sword's hilt

tsuri fishing rod

tsurube well bucket

tsutsu pipe

unagi eel

wagamono my thing (used

when refering to one's own penis)
yakkaibō troublesome stick
yanchabōzu naughty little boy
yari spear

yōbutsu sun thing
yōkon sun root
yoshiko (Yakuza slang)
yukei male stem
zun (Yakuza slang)
zundoko (Yakuza slang)

PENIS, erect

danbe (northwestern Japanese dialect origin)
gandaka goose high
gosun five *sun* (erect penis of over five inches)
hakebune sailboat
karidaka goose high

kōkachin from *kōka*, "stiff," and *chin*, "penis"
pinpin-chan little Mr. Boing-boing
rokusun six *sun* (erect penis of over six inches)

PENIS, impotent

akadama red ball (archaic)
burazō large, floppy organ
chōchin paper lantern
funyamara floppy penis
gifuchōchin lantern from Gifu
guzurōbe from *guzurō*, "slow," and the name-ending *be*

moderugan from the English "model gun" (looks potent, but does not work)
nankin soft balls
odawarachōchin lantern from Odawara
yowazō weak elephant
zō no hana elephant's trunk

PENIS, large

aodaishō blue-green snake
dekachin contraction of *deka*, "large," and *chinpo*, "penis"
dekamara from *deka*, "large," and *mara*, "penis"
itaname board licker (the

organ is so large, that when its owner is crouched down on his haunches at the bath the organ bounces down, "licking" the board)
itaneburi board licker (see *itaname*)

PENIS, large *(continued)*

konbō club
konebō kneading stick
kine pounder
magunamu magnum (student slang)
orochi monster serpent

uma horse (very large organ)
umaname horse lick (very large organ)
uwabami boa constrictor

PENIS, small

chinkoro (Osaka dialect origin)
chinmari snug
enptisu pencil
hari needle
hinedaikon shriveled radish (small, shriveled penis)
hosomi thin body
ikibari lively needle

kushi skewer
namekuji slug
nikubari meat needle
pākā Parker (college slang)
rōsoku candle
tanshō smallness
tōgarashi red pepper
waribashi wooden chopsticks

PENIS, special traits

guzurōbe slow and useless (impotent organ)
ibo pimple (organ with a thick torso and small head)
insatsumore printing error (organ without pubic hair)
inyake hidden burn (oversexed organ)
karakasa paper parasol (organ with large glans)
kasa umbrella (organ with large glans)
kibicho small underdeveloped organ (northeastern dialect origin)

rokei uncovered root (organ with short foreskin)
sakibuto tip thick (organ with large glans)
sanpachin organ that leans to the left when it is erect
sanpakei see *sanpachin*
subo tight (organ with long tight foreskin that does not recede during erection)
subomara tight penis (see *subo*)
utsubo moray eel (hairy penis)

PENIS, with long tight foreskin

fukuro sack
hamo sea eel
hitotsumenyudō one-eyed monster
hōkaburi kerchief
hōkamuri see *hōkaburi*
hōkei covered root
kawakaburi skin covered
kinukatsugi boiled taro root
menashibō eyeless stick
rakon exposed root
rakkyō scallion
rezāgan leather gun
rippustikku lipstick
suppon mud turtle

PIMP

aburamushi black beetle
akusoku bad leg
bohi inversion of *hibo*
dani tick (insect)
gokiburi cockroach
gyūtarō from *gyū*, "brothel tout"
hibo Osaka dialect verion of *himo*
himo rope
kyatchiman catch-man
manēja manager
Penisu no Shōnin The Merchant of Penis
ponbiki panderer
pōtā porter

POLICE

akapori red police (policewoman)
ahiru duck
ahōdori stupid bird, albatross
airōtsutsuai (ethnic Chinese origin)
aobuta blue pig (officer of the mobile unit)
aokarasu blue crow (officer of the mobile unit)
aokuri traffic policeman
aori stir up (undercover cop)
barikatotsuta (ethnic Korean origin)
barori pig (ethnic Korean origin)
biitenga (ethnic Chinese origin)
biyakutonkaru (ethnic Korean origin, Iksan city dialect)
bōfuri stick swinger
bu short for *bukei*
bukei inversion of *keibu*, "police inspector"
bukeiho inversion of *keibuho*, "assistant police inspector"

POLICE (continued)

buho short for *keibuho*, "assistant police inspector"

chāchiiyatsu (ethnic Chinese origin)

chari policeman on a bicycle

chiishuirā (ethnic Chinese origin)

chiyanbeku (ethnic Korean origin)

chonbu chiyanbeku (ethnic Korean origin)

chūhine middle gnarl (police section chief)

daikon megane radish with glasses (inexperienced, provincial policeman)

dani tick

deka (standard slang)

dekachō chief inspector

enma devil (Emma, king of the underworld)

enma-sama Lord Emma

en monkey

enii

etekō ape

gabinta barking dog (Korean origin, "no respect for one's superiors")

gacha clank

gokiburi cockroach (policeman on a motorcycle)

hachi bee

hayabusa falcon

hige beard

hime princess (police-woman)

hine gnarl

hoimu (ethnic Korean origin)

horudoki (ethnic Korean origin)

hoshi star

in'ya

inta

itachi weasel

itachō chief of police (from *itachi no chō*, "head of the weasels")

itakō

itashi

ite

itsunenanda detective (ethnic Korean origin)

itsuriyōchō detective (ethnic Korean origin)

jikei inversion of *keiji*, "detective"

jinkoro

kākō

kaku detective (from *kakusode*, "square sleeves," a pre-World War II word for "police-man in kimono")

kamaki (ethnic Korean origin)

kamaku (ethnic Korean origin)

kaminari thunderbolt

kamutai (Korean origin, Seoul dialect)

kanando

kanshiyoban (Korean origin)

karabakkari just the hull (ineffective policeman)

karasu crow (until a few years ago, policemen wore black uniforms)

karuchi uniformed officer (ethnic Korean origin)

karujichiyansakomoni (Korean origin)

kā-sama mommy

kata shape

kataoya shape dad (chief inspector)

kazaemon proper name

kazaguruma windmill

kazeguruma windmill

kē dog (ethnic Korean origin)

keisuke proper name

kejirami pubic louse

kijirushi devil's mark (mobile unit)

komucha (ethnic Korean origin)

konbo stick

koramatta from "Kora! Matta!" (Yo! Wait!), the words a policeman might shout out when he notices criminal activity going on (market slang)

kōtsu (ethnic Chinese origin)

koyani cat (ethnic Korean origin)

kingachiya

kuchiireya employment agency

kumo spider

kumōgi black color (ethnic Korean origin) (until a few years ago, Japanese policemen wore black uniforms)

kuri detective

kuriyama (market slang)

kyonchari from the Korean word for police, *kyongch'al*

maiki (ethnic Korean origin)

manbo

mappo

mōrin detective

mushi bug

nemusē (ethnic Korean origin, Kangwondo Chonwon dialect)

ningoro from *bannin*, "watchman," and *gorogoro*, "all over"

nioi smell

nozarubo field-monkey priest (archaic)

oa (ethnic Chinese origin)

obukei the honorific prefix "*o*," and *bukei*, an inversion of *keibu*, "police inspector"

ōbune ocean liner (chief of police)

odaishi saint

odeko forehead

oji uncle

POLICE (continued)

omakō contraction of om*awari-san*, "policeman," and *kō*, "dude"

omoya main building

ossan from *oji-san*, "uncle"

oyadama daddy bullet

oyahige daddy beard (chief detective)

oyahine daddy gnarl (chief detective)

oyaji old man

peruchiya (ethnic Korean origin)

pii-chan little Mr. P

porikoro

poriman shorter version of the English term "policewoman"

poruhaisha (ethnic Korean origin, Hamgyong Pukdo dialect)

rinhatsu (ethnic Chinese origin)

rōtsutsuai (ethnic Chinese origin)

rokutō (ethnic Korean origin)

sakubei proper name

sode sleeve

soppei quick fighter

suke bitch (policewoman)

surikogi wooden pestle

taikami (ethnic Korean origin)

taku (ethnic Korean origin)

tamu (ethnic Chinese origin)

tanko detective

tsuai (ethnic Chinese origin)

tsukina detective

udonya noodle vendor (bumbling, provincial policeman)

uo no tana fish shell

utori (ethnic Korean origin)

utsumatsujii detective (ethnic Korean origin)

wankō woof woof

yaba from *yabai*, "dangerous"

POLICE STATION

chitsuyau (ethnic Chinese origin)

chonbo (ethnic Korean origin)

hako box

kase from *tekase*, "handcuffs"

mokuchibu (ethnic Korean origin)

mugita (ethnic Korean origin)

mutsuku (ethnic Korean origin)

nokutsu (ethnic Korean origin)

piibii PB, for "police box"

piiesu PS, for "police station"

PRISON

asa from *yasa*, an inversion of *saya*, "sheath"

anbako dark box (detention center)

bakuan (ethnic Korean origin)

bessō villa

butabako pig box (detention center)

gachabako rattle box (detention center)

gamo short for "Sugamo prison"

honke real house

honmushi

hoteru hotel

ike pond

ikezoko bottom of a pond

kāriya (ethnic Chinese origin)

kamari detention ward

kinko safe

kiyachibu (Korean origin)

mushi six-four

mushiyoseba insect gathering place

nishikata

musho short for the standard word for "prison," *keimusho*

nyauyau (ethnic Chinese origin)

oyashiki mansion

renga brick

ryūchijo detention center

teihakukyo (ethnic Korean origin, Pukchong dialect)

teruho inversion of *hoteru*

uchi inside

yama mountain

yoseba gathering place

PRISON, warden

akaura red lining

chōkan governor

kanshu custodian (standard word)

oi hey!

oni devil

oyadoro from *oya*, "parent," and *doro*, "thief"

shukan inversion of *kanshu*, "custodian"

toantō (ethnic Chinese slang)

PROVINCIAL PERSON

imo potato (general slang)

imobēda pun on *imo*, "potato," and the English word "invader" (high school slang)

imo nē-chan potato sister (said of provincial women)

imo yarō potato guy

imo zoku potato gang

PROVINCIAL PERSON *(continued)*
(group of provincials)
imochi from *imo chippusu*, "potato chips" (high school slang)
potēto potato

korokke croquet (high school slang)
nagakō long guy
nakai (criminal slang)
notoshi (criminal slang)

PUBIC HAIR
bushu the English word "bush"
chinge male pubic hair (contraction of *chinpo*, "penis," and *ge*, "hair")
furungi (Okinawa dialect)
hēa the English word "hair" (popular slang)
hige beard
inmō hidden hair (standard slang)
insankaku hidden triangle
jinjiroge
jinjirage (northwestern Japanese dialect origin)
ke hair (popular slang)
keba hair feathers

kebu (northeastern Japanese dialect origin)
kebuko (northeastern Japanese dialect origin)
keburi
mange female pubic hair (contraction of *manko*, "vagina," and *ge*, "hair")
mitsurin jungle
otoge (southern Japanese dialect origin)
sankaku triangle
tsubihige woman's pubic hair (from *tsubi*, "vagina" and *hige*, "beard")
yabu bush

RAZOR
atarigane suave metal
ate also means "blade of a knife"
gamu gum (when you buy a razor, it is wrapped up

like gum)
sakai edge
sori short for *kamisori*, "razorblade"
suri from *sori*

SEXUAL INTERCOURSE
aikagi awasu fitting the master key in the lock

anmoku tacit permission
doreiai

bikuhiku

biri

bukkomu to drive into

esu the initial S, short for "sex"

etchi suru to do H (which stands for *hentai*, "perversion")

hamekomu to plunge in

hameru to put in

heguru

heppe (northern Japanese dialect origin)

inko

kanraku merriment, pleasure

kamari slithering in

keai cock fight (pun on *ke ai*, "pubic hair encounter")

ken de moru

senrei baptism

sumō Japanese sumo wrestling

sutanpu stamp

tsubi (northern Japanese dialect origin)

tsuboyaki pot burning

tsukkomu to thrust in

tsukimakkuru to stab again and again

yachi o fuku wiping the cunt

zukon bakon zap bang (onomatopoeic)

SPERM

bitamin esu vitamin S (high school slang)

esu the initial S, short for "sperm" (also used to mean "sex")

gyūnyū milk

karupisu from the milky Japanese soft drink "Calpis"

kodanejiru child-seed soup

miruku the English word "milk"

nori glue

nurunuru slimy

otokojiru male soup

otokonyūeki male milky lotion

rabujūsu the English word "love juice"

shasei ejaculation (standard word)

seieki semen (standard word)

supanku the British English slang expression "spunk"

sūpu the English word "soup"

toro from *torori*, "thick liquid"

tsuyu juice

yōguruto the English word "yogurt"

zāmen from the German word *Samen*, "seed"

TAMPON

banira vanilla (as in "vanilla-ice cone")
kuraka cracker

tii baggu tea bag
wairesumaiku wireless microphone

TATTOO

gaman patience
kanban placard
kurikaramonmon large elaborate tattoo

monmon from *kurikaramonmon*
sumi from *irezumi*, "tattoo"

TELEPHONE

rinrin ring ring
tere short for *terefuon*, "telephone"

tsunagi connection
waden inversion of *denwa*, "telephone"

TESTICLES

bōru the English word "balls"
chintama from *chin*, "penis," and *tama*, "balls" (also used for "penis")
danbe (southwestern Japanese dialect origin)
dango rice cake
dara tobacco pouch (Hiroshima dialect origin)
donben (Nagasaki area origin)
fugui (used in southern Japan and Okinawa)
fuguri testicle sack (street slang)
fuinukunga the eggs

(*kunga*) of the penis (*fui*) (Okinawa slang)
funguri from *fuguri*, "testicle sack"
funguidani (Okinawa, Yonagunijima dialect origin)
furudani (Okinawa slang)
goro (southern Japanese dialect origin)
heppe (criminal jargon, northern Japanese dialect origin)
hetsuguri (street slang, Niigata dialect origin)
hōju precious gem (priest slang)
hōma (criminal jargon)
kaite (criminal jargon)

kinkuri (Shizuoka dialect origin)

kinta short for *kintama* (Amami Oshima dialect in southern Japan)

kintama golden balls (standard slang)

kintare golden dangle (criminal jargon, Hiroshima dialect origin)

kintsū (street slang expression used in southern Japanese cities, Hiroshima dialect origin)

kōma egg (Okinawa dialect slang)

kuga egg (Okinawa dialect slang)

kūga from *kuga*, "egg"

kyappe (Yakuza slang)

kyōheki large treasure-balls (priest slang)

ohagi rice dumplings covered with bean jam

oinarisan type of sushi that originated in Osaka

oinaribukuro roundish sack of deep fried tofu into which sushi is stuffed

pugui (Okinawa island slang)

ryōgaku spiritual balls (priest slang)

sunbako (northern Japanese dialect origin)

suzuko bell child (northern Japanese dialect origin)

tagu (Kagoshima dialect origin)

taimo (Osaka origin)

tama balls (standard slang)

tane seed (southen Japanese dialect origin)

tani seed (Okinawa dialect origin)

tansu rice cake (Toyama dialect origin)

TESTICLES, special traits

doben pot, large testicles (Southern Japanese dialect origin)

dobenoko large, low-hanging testicles (Nagasaki slang)

dobin from *doben*, "pot"

donbi large testicles (criminal jargon, central Japanese dialect origin)

katafuri side hang (one testicle hangs lower than the other)

katakin side gold (northern Japanese dialect origin)

kenke pickles (small, tight testicles, central Japanese dialect origin)

ochin small testicles, child's testicles (Osaka dialect origin)

ufufuri large testicles

TESTICLES, special traits *(continued)*

(Ishigaki, Okinawa slang)

unguiteii small testicles

(Yonagunijima island slang)

TOILET

akuba foul place
heya room
kasetto the English word "cassette" (pun inspired by the Japanese for "the sound enters" *oto ire*, which is homophonous to *otoire*, "toilet")
kenkeya shit house
kusobeya shit room
kusodokoro shit place

kusonba shit place
kusoya shit house
mokukan (ethnic Korean origin)
oura the honorific particle "*o*," and *ura*, "back"
samuchibori (ethnic Korean origin)
shianjo place of reflection
suteba dumping ground
ura back

URINATING

bibi (high school slang)
jūroku sixteen (pun on *shi shi*, which can mean "four fours")
kozume small press
oshikko pee pee (standard slang)

shiiko (northern dialect version of *oshikko*)
shishi wee wee
shonbe (Harima dialect version of *shōben*)
shōsui small water

URINATING, men

tachishōben standing piss

tsutsuharai shaking the tube

URINATING, women

gōu downpour
manshon contraction of *man*, "cunt," and *shōben*,

"piss"
teppō mizu flash flood
yūdachi sudden shower

VAGINA

agura squatting, sitting crosslegged

akagai ark shell

akasubori red squeeze

akamon red gate

akamonmon from *akamon*

akamunmun from *akamon*

akebi akebi fruit

amaguri roasted chestnut

amidanyorai Amithaba (priest slang)

ana hole

anabachi hole pot

asoko over there

baimo shell mother

bakagai surf clam (literally "fool's shell")

bappe (northern Japanese dialect origin)

bebe (southern Japanese dialect origin)

becho (*bechō*) (northeastern Japanese dialect origin)

bekya (northern Japanese dialect origin)

betcho (northeastern Japanese dialect origin)

bii

biibā beaver

biku fish trap

bo Kobe slang

bobo standard slang (southern Japanese origin)

bobojo (southern Japanese dialect origin)

bocho (southern Japanese dialect origin)

bokkusu the English word "box" (student slang)

cha from *chiya*, the inversion of *yachi*, "bog"

chacha (western Japanese dialect origin)

chako (northern Japanese dialect origin)

chancha (western Japanese dialect origin)

chanko (northern Japanese dialect origin)

chatsubo tea canister

chia from *chiya*, an inversion of *yachi*

chibi small thing, tiny gadget

chikin chicken (student slang)

chiya inversion of *yachi*

cho (northern Japanese dialect origin)

chonko

dappe (northern Japanese dialect origin)

deruta delta

deruta chitai delta zone

emeru pun on *emu*, which means both "smile" and "crack"

enko

fuigo bellows

fuiku the English word "fig"

fuji-san Mount Fuji

fukube gourd

fukubebiri tail end

fune ship

VAGINA *(continued)*

furusato birthplace

gama toad

gamaguchi toad's mouth, wallet

gen

hachi bowl

hako box

hama beach

hamehame jab jab

happe (northern Japanese dialect origin)

hehe (northern Japanese dialect origin)

heki cleft

heko (hekko) (northern Japanese dialect origin)

heppe (Hokkaido dialect origin)

hikeshitsubo charcoal extinguisher

hizō treasure

hobo (northern dialect version of *bobo*)

horagai trumpet shell

ichi

ichi no tani the first valley

ichi o osu press one

ichijiku fig

ichiki

ike pond

ikimi breathing body

inoshishi wild boar

inrō pill box

iwato rock door

kai shell

kanete

kani crab

kannon Goddess of Mercy

kanū canoe

keburo hairy tub

kebuton hairy futon

kegani hairy crab

kegawa fur

keman contraction of *ke*, "hair," and *omanko*, "vagina"

kemanjū hairy bean-jam bun

kemaru hairy zero

kemomo hair peach

kiiga inversion of *gakki*, "musical instrument"

kinchaku leather pouch

kippin lucky object

kizu gash

kobako small box

kokyō native place

kubo hollow, sunken depression

kubomi pit

kuma ana bear hole

kurebasu crevice (student slang)

kurēta crater (student slang)

kuromono black thing

mito

maeana front hole

maejiri front ass

maku no uchi behind the curtains

mame bean

mamezō from *mame*, "bean," and the Japanese name-ending *zō*

manjū bean-jam bun

(southern Japanese
    dialect origin)
manko (Shikoku island
    origin)
mehi inversion of *hime*,
    "princess"
meicho (southern Japanese
    dialect origin)
meiki exquisite article
meko (Shikoku island
    origin)
meme (southern Japanese
    dialect origin)
meme-jo (southern Japa-
    nese dialect origin)
meme-ko (southern
    Japanese dialect origin)
meme-san (southern
    Japanese dialect origin)
menko (western Japanese
    dialect origin)
miiman one's own vagina
    (combination of the
    English "me" and *man*,
    "vagina")
mitto (street slang)
momo peach
mon gate
moyamoya no seki hairy
    barrier
mukimi stripped shellfish
nabe cookpot
naijin inside person
namagai raw shell
nikuburo meat tub
nikutsubo meat jar
nukabukuro rice-bran bag
numa swamp
obake ghoul

ocha tea
ochanko (northern Japanese
    dialect origin)
ochawan tea bowl
ochaire teapot
ochatsubo teapot
ohachi pot, rice tub
ohako box
oka hill
okaigai shell shell
okame Kabuki theater mask
okunoin the holy of holies,
    the inner sanctum
okuromono black thing
    (from *kuromono*)
oma (central Japanese
    origin)
omanko (standard slang,
    northern and central
    Japanese origin)
omanman (student slang)
omatsuri festival
ome (Kobe slang)
omecha (Hiroshima dialect
    origin)
omecho (omechō) (Hiro-
    shima dialect origin)
omeko (standard slang,
    central and southern
    Japanese origin)
omencha (Hiroshima
    dialect origin)
omencho (omenchō) (Hiro-
    shima dialect origin)
omenko (western Japanese
    dialect origin)
omonmon (student slang)
omotemon front gate
omunmun (student slang)

VAGINA *(continued)*

onkoto merciful thing
osugata shape
pi (Okinawa dialect)
pii (ethnic Chinese origin, possibly from *mao-pii*, "fur")
pushii pussy
reishi litchi fruit
renge lotus
rōzu rose (student slang)
ryūfā mahjong pawn
saikuba workshop
sakazuki goblet
sato short for *furusato*, "birthplace"
saya sheath
seribako competitive box
shansu (ethnic Chinese origin)
shijimi corbicula shell
shimegi oil press
shimo down
shimonoseki lower gate
shinzō bride
shita down
shitaba lower place
shitakuchi lower mouth
shumon orange gate
soso (standard slang)
suiden rice paddy
suika watermelon

sumitsubo ink pot
suribachi earthenware mortar
suritto slit
tako octopus
tachiusu standing vase
tani valley
tatsuware vertical slit
tsubi from *chibi*, "small thing"
tsubo canister
tsunbi (Shizuoka dialect version of *tsubi*)
umarezaisho birthplace
umeboshi pickled plum
usu mortar
uri melon
utsuwa utensil
waraji straw sandals
wareme-chan little Miss Crack (student slang)
yachi bog, swamp
yage
yagen mortar used to crush drugs
yake short for *yakeku*
yakeku
yajibako heckling box
yakihamaguri baked clam
yohamaguri night clam

VAGINA, medieval

aoda blue field
ama no iwato heaven's stone door
ashiwara reed field

bokka wooden melon
funadama-sama guardian deity of a ship
hinado princess's door

hoto hearth (Nara period)
horagai trumpet shell
ichimangoku
ikigai living shell
keginchaku hair purse
kesetta hairy sandals
kewaraji hairy straw
   sandals
nada open sea
okinoishi rock in the sea

okōbako incense box
onokizu
sora sky
shakogai clam shell
tachikizu sword wound
takenoko bamboo shoot
tani valley
tare woman's head
waraji straw sandals
yachi bog

VAGINA, special traits

akanabe red cookpot
   (menstruating organ)
ama nun (shaved pubic
   region; Japanese nuns
   shave their heads)
anaguma hole bear (hairy
   pubic region)
donabe mud pot (provincial
   woman's organ)
cherii furawā cherry flower
   (virginal organ)
furo bathtub (large organ)
furōke bathtub (large
   organ)
karasukai raven shell (the
   hairy pubic region of a
   mature woman)
kegawa hair skin (hairy
   pubic region)
kawarake unglazed earthen
   cup (shaved organ)
kinchaku vagina with
   strong muscle wall
kizumono broken thing
   (deflowered organ)
nikuburo meat tub (large

vagina)
obenko virginal organ
   (northern Japanese
   dialect origin)
ochoko sake bowl (small
   organ)
ohachi rice tub (large
   organ)
osara narrow dish (tight or
   shallow organ)
ōzara platter (large organ)
otoshiana pitfall (large
   organ)
pinku pink (virginal organ)
saragai new shell (virginal
   organ)
sekohan secondhand
   (deflowered organ)
shijimi corbicular shell
   (small organ)
shiofuki surf clam (small
   organ)
suika no tanaochi melon that
   fell off the shelf (sexual
   organ of an unattractive
   elderly woman)

VAGINA, special traits *(continued)*

todana cupboard (large organ)

yachihakui bog in white

(accomplished organ of a mature woman)

WALLET

bochi

bōgara empty wallet

chinkichi

dainomono

fukuro bag

fusai reverse of *saifu*, "wallet"

gamaguchi frog's mouth

hitsujiire sheep entrance

hōza (Korean origin)

ike buried

iwa rock

iwagara from *iwa kara*, "the rock is empty" (empty wallet)

jinsuke

kaeru frog

kaerudachi frog's friend

kobayashi

mosa gut

mosagara from *mosa kara*, "the gut is empty" (empty wallet)

miire money inside a wallet

namaire from *nama*, "raw" or "cash," and *ire*, "entry"

nakasuki pull out from within (some cliques use this to refer to wallets, others to pockets)

nasu eggplant

nakanuki extract from inside

nuki extract

pāsu from the English word "purse"

roppuku money inside a wallet

sai from *saifu*, "wallet"

suirai torpedo

tai base

umo

yoichi

yoichibā

yū

zuda short for *zudabukuro*, "wallet"